Medieval Folk Tales for Children

Medieval Folk Tales for Children

Dave Tonge

Illustrated by Kim Voisey

The History Press

For my friend, mentor and fellow yarnsmith, Stewart Alexander, and also all the other storytellers who have kept these stories alive over the past 1,000 years.

First published 2020

The History Press
97 St George's Place, Cheltenham,
Gloucestershire GL50 3QB
www.thehistorypress.co.uk

British Library Cataloguing in Publication Data.
A catalogue record for this book is available from the British Library.

ISBN 978 0 7509 9094 3

Typesetting and origination by The History Press
Printed in Europe

Contents

Thank Yous

Big thank yous to Helen James for proof-reading my work and to my young friends Tal Fee, Althea Broughton-Squire and Poppy Hall and their parents, Poppy and Curtis Fee, Su Squire and Alison Hurd for their expert opinions on children's stories. Thanks also to Suzanne Arnold for her continued support and encouragement. And a very huge thank you to Kim Voisey for her marvellously medieval illustrations. Kimmy – you rock!

About the Author

Dave is a professional storyteller who travels all over England telling his tales. History was his favourite subject at school, so he thinks himself very lucky that he can dress up like a Saxon, medieval or Tudor storyteller and tell tales in ancient castles and at ruined medieval priories. The very first story he ever told was one adapted from *The Canterbury Tales*, a collection of medieval stories written by Geoffrey Chaucer. It's a story about three foolish young men and Death and it's included right here in his book.

About the Illustrator

Kim teaches art at City College Norwich. She loves the early mornings, her dog, Pilgrim, and also history, and based the illustrations for this book on 'illuminated manuscripts', meaning decorated medieval writings like the Luttrell and Macclesfield Psalters. They are religious books, yet most of the pictures used to decorate them are of people working on the land, drinking in alehouses, dancing to music and having fun. And Kim really loves to have fun!

About This Book

Welcome to my book of medieval folk tales. Before we get to the stories, I want you to imagine that I'm offering you a white feather, perhaps from a goose like the one pictured above. But what if I was to tell you that it was actually a feather from an angel's wing; a religious relic, meaning an object with almost magical powers that could cure you of any illness and bring you good luck? Many of you would not believe me, yet if you had lived in medieval times most of you would, even paying me silver coins to buy the feather for yourselves. We live in a world of the internet and education, of knowledge of how the world works. We live in a time where death and disease are kept at bay by science and medicines, but medieval people were not so lucky. They could not expect to live as long as we do and often they died in horrible ways: from violent wars to deadly diseases like the Black Death. And so, by going to church and on pilgrimage to visit the tombs of godly saints and also by believing in religious relics like the angel's feather, medieval people had some hope of a better life.

Their lives were ruled by religion and to break the Church's rules was to commit a sin, bad behaviour that could send you to Purgatory when you died, a place where you would be terribly tortured, at least that's what the Church said, long ago. Churchmen spoke of seven deadly sins – envy, gluttony, lust, sloth, pride, greed and wrath – and they found their way into many a folk tale. And know that these stories came in all different shapes and sizes when they were told by troubadours and jongleurs, the storytellers of long ago. Some were legends of the Celtic peoples who lived here before medieval times. Some of the stories came over to England after the Norman Conquest and were called 'romances' and 'chansons de geste', which is French for 'songs of deeds'. They were long stories about brave knights, but there were also much shorter magical tales called 'Breton lays'. Others were 'fables' about animals, which were sometimes used by the Church to teach people right from wrong. But medieval folk also enjoyed comic tales about farts and other rude things, called 'fabliaux' and 'jests', and I have included examples of all these different types of tales in my book.

Many of the stories were already old when they arrived here in medieval times. Ancient collections like *The Seven Wise Masters* came from faraway places like India and Persia. They were translated from foreign languages by monks and other learned medieval folk into new books like the *Gesta Romanorum*, which is Latin for *The Deeds of the Romans*. And during that time the stories changed, especially when medieval writers began mixing old tales together to make new ones. Two of the most famous writers to do this were Geoffrey Chaucer in his *Canterbury Tales* and the Italian Giovanni Boccaccio in his *Decameron*. Both Boccaccio and Chaucer used 'framing narratives', meaning big stories in which other tales were told. In Chaucer the frame story was about a group of pilgrims travelling to Canterbury to visit the tomb of Saint Thomas Becket, taking it in turns to tell tales to entertain the others. In Boccaccio's book the main story was about a group of young people who escaped to the hills above the city of Florence while the Black Death killed many below, and there they shared stories to pass the time. You can find out more about the medieval story collections I've used in the bibliography at the end of my book, and there is also a glossary that explains some of the older and more unusual words that I like to use in my tales. Think of it as a modern version of a knightly quest, a medieval adventure where you must seek out secret wisdom! Although not all the knowledge is hidden, for each chapter starts with a nugget of history about the medieval kings who ruled England. They were believed to have a God-given right to rule, but as you'll see, they had just as many faults as the rest of us!

And so at last we are coming to the stories. Each of them ends with a rhyme, a reminder that many a medieval storyteller like Chaucer set down their stories in verse. Unlike Chaucer, I haven't included a frame story with my collection, although there is nothing to stop you imagining that you are part of a bigger tale – perhaps listening to my stories as you ride out on a beautiful spring morning, the cool rains giving way to bright sunshine, while the buzz of busy bees about the blossom accompanies each tale. Or perhaps you would prefer to be relaxing with friends on an Italian hillside, lying in the dappled shade of some

ancient twisted tree while gazing out over the warm red-tiled roofs and richly decorated churches of Florence. You might yearn to be in a faraway king's sumptuous palace surrounded by rich lords and ladies dressed in fine furs and soft silks. Or maybe you would prefer the company of rough-hewn folk, the poorer people gathered together in the village alehouse enjoying good food and even better company, laughing their aches and ailments away for a while at least. Whatever your choice, know that the storyteller is about to tell the first of many tales and he starts as so many medieval troubadours did long ago…
'Harken unto my words, listen and hold your tongues, for I have a tale to tell.'

1

When the Anglo-Saxon King of England, Edward the Confessor, died, he had no children of his own and so promised the throne of England to many rulers from other lands – from Harold Hardrada, King of Norway to Duke William of Normandy, his distant cousin. Yet it was Harold Godwinson, the most powerful of all Edward's Saxon earls, who was envious of the power of kings and so took the throne for his own. But Duke William of Normandy also looked upon the riches of England with envious eyes and so attacked England, beating the Anglo-Saxons at the Battle of Hastings in 1066. And so it was that he became King William I of England and it is his rule that for me marks the beginning of the medieval period and the beginning of my book.

***Envy** means to want something that someone else has so badly and to hate them because they have more than you. It was thought to be a very dangerous sin in medieval times, for it could lead to violence and even murder…*

Of Fire in the Fens

There were many bold outlaws in medieval times, from Fulk Fitzwarin to Robin Hood. Yet a father to them all was Hereward the Wake. His story came first and, unlike Robin Hood, Hereward was a real man whose life became legend, a blending together of truth and lies… For once, in the fens of East Anglia long ago, there lived a Saxon called Hereward, who found fame for his wakeful, watchful ways. Some called him a hero, but others whispered that he was a base-born thief who was jealous of richer, more famous men. Even his own father was angered by Hereward's evil behaviour and cast the boy from his halls.

But Hereward thrived upon the hatred of others, for he was full of rage and fire and sought only to prove that he was a brave and powerful man in the making. And so it was that he travelled to Northumbria, where he found fame slaying a giant bear, a man-eating bloodstained beast. Then he journeyed into Cornwall and did battle with a cruel tyrant called Rough Scab, a fine name don't you think, my friends? Beating him in battle, Hereward took the tyrant's sword and renamed it Brain-biter, a name that in time would make his many enemies quake.

Well, with so many heroic deeds to his name, it is not surprising that when the Norman duke, William, conquered this land, our sturdy hero was not here to fight against him. But when Hereward returned to these shores he grew angry at the greed of his new masters. Normans lorded it over all, stripping the land and the people of their wealth. In his own boyhood home Hereward watched as the new Norman abbot of St Peter's Abbey demanded more tithes and taxes from the poor Saxons,

a people who had no more to give. Hereward the Wake grew so angry that he gathered together a rebel gang, men like Leofric the Mower who was armed with a scythe, a curved blade normally used for cutting crops. And with his Saxon warriors Hereward attacked the abbey, stealing all that glittered and was gold; be it coin, candlestick or chalice, he took it all, claiming that he was keeping it from greedy, grasping Norman hands.

But our hero's actions brought him no satisfaction, his deeds lay heavy upon the wakeful warrior. And on the night of the day that he had attacked the abbey the darkest of dreams rose up within Hereward, just as the chill damp mists rose up from the marshes that surrounded his fenland home. For in his sleep an old man came to Hereward, an old man with a bent back and a beard so long that it dusted the floor, while his face was lined by misery and woe. It was Saint Peter from the Heavens above and he was searching for all that our Saxon outlaw had stolen, crying out, 'Why, Hereward? Why?' Hereward awoke with a start, his mood as dark as the short and darkening days of the season, his heart as grey and grim as the grim and grey winter's day breaking without. He realised that his fight was with the Normans and not with the saints in Heaven above.

Hereward ordered his men to return the abbey's treasure and then mounted his horse, a swift mare called Swallow, and with his sword, Brain-biter, in his hand, the brave outlaw and his burly band came smashing and crashing out of the fenland fogs, falling upon carts loaded with Norman gold. And Brain-biter was true to its name, for the fens were stained red with Norman blood. For what could the Normans do? They were defeated by the Saxons' homeland as ever they were by their swords and axes. The boggy fens swallowed Norman knights and horses whole and the Saxons were as slippery and elusive as any eel that swam in the rivers that snaked across their land. So too the Normans were fearful of the bogarts and other foul fenland fairies that dwelt in that dark foreboding place, cruel creatures who fed upon the fear of men.

Well, know, my friends, that just as stories of bogarts grew in the telling, so too did Hereward's tale grow as it was shared among his friends and enemies alike. Such was his infamy that it reached the ears of the Conqueror, King William, whose anger was legend. Having already put down a Saxon rebellion in the north of England, he would not flinch from destroying all those who challenged him in our hero's fenland home. The Norman king sent his spies into the wetlands and soon he heard tell that Hereward's stronghold was

on an island surrounded by marsh – and since he was not coming out, then William and his soldiers would have need to go in.

He raised a great bridge across water and marsh and many Saxons were forced to break their backs, building the great wooden road. But while most hated the work, other Saxons did not, for Hereward and his fearsome friends came disguised with hoods, hats and cloaks. With mallet, maul and axe they helped to fell trees, to sink huge wooden posts into the marshy land, to split logs into planks and to nail them to the giant bridge. And as its stout, sturdy towers grew tall, so too Hereward's plans grew large, for all the time he was wakeful and watchful of all that was going on.

Well so it was, the causeway was complete when William arrived with an army at his back, bringing with him an old witch who was as ugly within as she was without, while her hatred for Saxons was only matched by her love of Norman gold! King William hoped that the Saxons would be fearful of the dark magic that followed the old woman wherever she went and that she would drive them all from their island fortress in terror. And so the king set her to work, shrieking shrilly from one of the bridge's many towers as his army marched on the wooden causeway below. There she stood, calling, casting and cackling her spells, baring her bony backside and beating a drum, crying out,

> I curse you Saxons, for you have all fallen upon Dame Fortune's wheel, never to rise again. Your luck drains from your battle-weary bodies and drips into the murky mud that will be your graves. My rats have scuttled over your bodies and gnawed at your tattered clothes while

> you slept and the worms wait in the dark, damp, dank earth beneath to feast upon your foul flesh!

But while the witch wailed and many a frightened Norman soldier paled at the wild woman's wicked words, Hereward and his men were rowing on rafts, going quickly and quietly from pile to post beneath the wooden causeway, painting the heavy timbers with pig fat and pitch. Then with flaming torches they set the causeway alight, before rowing back into the misty marshland from whence they came. The bold hero looked back only once at the old crone, still calling, cackling and cursing all Saxons, yet now her eyes glimmered in the darkness, telling him that his work was well done; the causeway was ablaze!

Over two hundred Norman soldiers ran thither and yon, many leaping into the dark icy waters that would be their doom, as the flames rose up high around the wooden towers, feasting upon the newly felled timbers. Yet the fire's hunger was not easily satisfied and now it sought to dine upon human flesh, for as the witch wailed, the fire consumed her, so too the Norman soldiers who clung woebegone and whimpering to the causeway's burnt and blackened beams.

Ash and burning embers danced on the wind as the blazing towers sunk beneath the marshy mire and the old woman's shrill shrieks were replaced by the hiss of steam and eventually silence. The Norman king and all that was left of his army marched away, never to return to Hereward's fenland home. But perhaps, my friends, he did not need to, for although our brave Saxon outlaw won this battle, it was King William the Conqueror who won the war.

The outlaw was wakeful and watched
over all,
The witch she was wicked and in flames
she did fall.

Of Medicine and Murder

If you fell sick in medieval times and had money you might send for a physician, what they called a doctor long ago… For once there was an old physician who could treat many a medieval illness that ailed men and brought women low. Such was the doctor's fame that a clever student asked the old man to train him in medicine, offering to pay the physician for his lessons. The old doctor agreed and the young student learnt fast, quickly becoming a finer physician than his master. It was soon said of the young student that he could cure his patients' boils and their belly aches, their colds and contagions, their sorrows and their sores. Such was the young man's skill that the

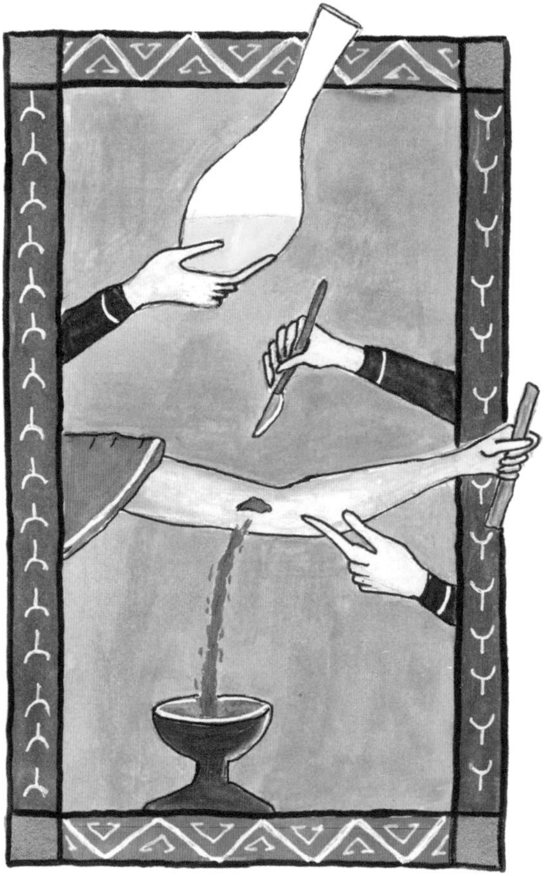

old doctor grew jealous of his student and envious of his fame.

Well, one day a king's messenger arrived from a faraway land and asked the old doctor to go with him, for the king's son was so sick he was close to death. It was a dreadful disease that no other physician could cure, no matter what they tried. Some had studied the prince's urine, his pee held high to the light in a glass. Some tried bleeding the boy, thinking his blood was bad, but taking so much that he grew sicker still. Others made the prince breathe in the fumes of burning feathers and other foul odours, hoping to drive the deadly disease away. But as I'm sure you all know, my friends, such terrible treatments had no effect and that was why the messenger came for the old doctor. He was the king's last and only hope.

But the old doctor would not go with the messenger, for he had heard that the king was a cruel man who would punish anyone who allowed the boy to die. Instead, he sent his young student, for he had grown to hate the lad and hoped that he would fail and so never come home. But the clever young physician did not fail, for quickly he cured the prince of his ills and such was the king's joy that he rewarded the student with many riches and sent him home a wealthy man.

Well, if the old doctor was jealous before, now his envy became a seething rage. No sooner had the student returned home than his mean-minded master took him into the woods to pick herbs and roots to make medicines, for their stores were getting low. Deeper into the woods they went until they came to a patch of worts, simple flowers used to make creams that could soothe many a burn and rash. 'Look here,' said the old doctor, 'a fine flower right by my feet. If you pick it for me, I'll teach you of all the ailments that this wondrous plant can treat.' The student did as his master asked, but no sooner did he bend low than the old man struck him with an oaken log, killing the young man stone dead. Quickly he buried the lad's body beneath leaf, twig and dirt, and told everyone that the student had returned to serve the king whose son he had cured.

The old doctor had got rid of his clever young rival, and I bet some of you are thinking, 'Hang on, that's not fair!' But wait, my friends, there is a little more to tell. For not long after, the old doctor fell ill with the same deadly disease that had struck down the prince in the land far away. The old doctor tried to cure himself, but could not and so he paid other physicians to save him. Some studied the old man's urine, held high to the light in a glass. Some tried bleeding the old doctor, but took so much blood that the he grew sicker still. Others made him breathe in burning feathers and other foul odours, hoping to drive the deadly disease away. But nothing worked. 'I have done all I can,' said each doctor in turn, 'and so you must send for your student, for he is the only one who can save you now.' But as you and I know, the envious old physician could not ask the lad's help and so he died a broken and withered man.

The old doctor did kill and for that he paid,
For now there was no one to come to his aid.

Of Some Midwinter Magic

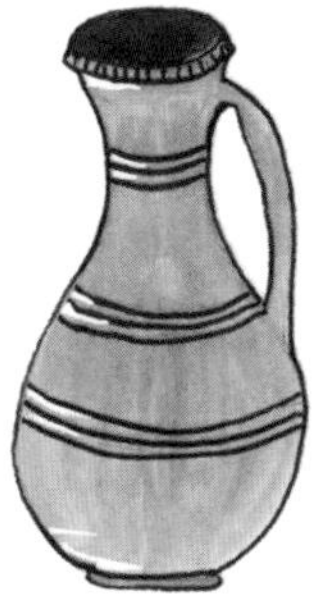

Medieval knights were expected to be brave in battle, but the rules of chivalry that they were supposed to follow also said that they must be kind and generous to others – for once, there lived a knight called Sir Cleges, who never slew a dragon, nor even a brutal boar. Know, my friends, that brave feats upon the battlefield he did few and yet still he won great fame for both his wisdom and generous nature. Largesse is what they called it in medieval times, munificence and hospitality too. For Sir Cleges always kept roaring fires and soft feather mattresses for footsore, weary travellers and a full larder for his own hungry vassals, the medieval men and women who worked on his lands.

So great was the old knight's generous reputation that strangers came from far and wide to sample his charity, and so, as my story starts, it finds Sir Cleges made poor by his own hospitable ways. He had nothing more to give, not even to his own wife and children. Worse still, it was winter, a time of great dearth when little or nothing grows through the cold, frozen earth. And this winter was particularly cruel, for it wrapped itself around the country like a great icy cloak, while its long, bitter fingers reached deep inside the people and tickled their ribs, chilling them to the bone. It was a wicked winter that found the Sir Cleges in low spirits, for now it was Christmas Eve, when noble lords had a duty to provide fine feasts, and what would his vassals think of him now that his tables were bare? The old knight wandered his snow-covered garden and was inclined to grumble at his ill-deserved fate.

But Sir Cleges's wife came into the garden and chided him, reminding the old knight that although he was no longer able to provide food and other comforts, he was still able to give his family love. For, unlike the wood for their fires and meat for their bellies, his love should never run short. She offered her downcast husband a simple drink made from the juice of the cherry, all that they had left now that others had drunk their best wine. Sir Cleges thanked his wife for her wise words, telling her to go and get warm and that he would join his family when he had walked his woes and worries away. And so it was that he went alone into his orchard and stood among the frostbitten cherry trees. And as he stood silently pondering his problems, he remembered how in times past the people would give something back to the earth as thanks for the harvest and as an offering to ensure an even better one in the year to come. Sir Cleges knelt before the oldest cherry tree and spoke these simple words: 'Cherry tree, cherry tree, what you have given unto me, I will give back unto thee.' And then he cast the cherry juice over the gnarled and knotted roots and bowed his head in silent prayer.

As the old knight knelt in front of the old cherry tree, a drop of icy water fell upon his neck, making him jump and, looking up, he saw that although snow still covered most of the garden, it no longer touched his cherry trees. Before his eyes there appeared green

shoots, then blossom and finally cherries. Miraculous midwinter cherries, fresh-grown in the middle of a cruel and hard winter at that! Sir Cleges and his vassals picked every last one and all feasted upon cherry pie, cherry cake and cherry liquor, a drink so strong that it made everyone forget their many winter worries and woes.

But know, my friends, there is only so much enjoyment to be had from cherries, fine though they be, and so the old knight decided he would take a cartload of his miraculous midwinter fruit to his old friend and master, King Uther Pendragon, hoping for a rich reward. And so it was that Sir Cleges, dressed in his oldest clothes for the journey and with a sturdy staff in hand, set forth on his travels. The road was long and rutted by horse hoof and cart wheel, full of puddles filled with melting snow and ice, and the generous knight met plenty of poor folk in need of food. He parted with many of his cherries – so many, in fact, that by the time he reached Uther's castle, he had but one basketful left. But it did not matter, for he knew the king would still be amazed by his gift of miraculous midwinter cherries, fresh-grown in the middle of a cruel and hard winter at that!

But Sir Cleges's weary walk was written upon his lined and haggard face, and in his old and ragged clothes he looked more like a beggar than the noble knight that we all know him to have been. He knocked loudly with his staff against the bailey gate, the first of many gateways that pierced the stone defences of Uther's castle keep. Sir Cleges continued knocking until at last Uther's constable, an envious man who was in charge of all the king's castles, looked out of a small window set within the wooden door. Seeing only an old beggar standing there, who clearly had nothing to offer him, he threatened to cut off his nose if he did not leave. 'Be off with you, roguish rascal,' shouted he. And so it was that Sir Cleges opened the basket so that the constable might see the gift he had brought. And when the greedy servant looked inside, his eyes lit up – miraculous midwinter cherries, fresh-grown in the middle of a cruel and hard winter at that! He thought to himself, 'For such a wondrous gift, the king is sure to reward this old beggar with an equally wonderful prize,' and being an envious man, he wanted his share. He would let the old beggar pass through the gate, but only if he agreed to give the constable one third of any reward that King Uther gave unto him.

Well, Sir Cleges agreed, even though it meant that he would only get two thirds of any reward that the king offered. But being a noble man, he kept his temper and continued on his way, until he came to another gate at the bottom of the great stone steps that led up to Uther's great stone castle keep. Sir Cleges beat hard upon the door until at last the steward, a jealous man who controlled the king's household, looked out of a small window set into the wooden door. Seeing only an old beggar standing there, who clearly had nothing to offer him, he threatened to cut off his ears if he did not leave. 'Be off with you, vile villain,' shouted he. And so it was that Sir Cleges opened the basket so that the steward might see the gift he had brought. And when the greedy servant looked inside, his eyes lit up – miraculous midwinter cherries, fresh-grown in the middle of a cruel and hard winter at that! He thought to himself, 'For such a wondrous gift, the king is sure to reward this old beggar with an equally wonderful prize,' and being a jealous man, he wanted his share. He would let the old beggar pass through the gate, but only if he agreed to give the steward one third of any reward that King Uther gave unto him.

Well, Sir Cleges agreed, even though it meant that he would only get one third of any reward that the king offered. But being a noble man, he kept his temper and continued on his way, climbing the great stone steps and beat on the great oak door that led into Uther's great hall. He continued knocking until at last the chamberlain, a covetous man who controlled the king's coin, looked out of a small window set into the wooden door. Seeing only an old beggar standing there, who clearly had nothing to offer him, he threatened to put out his eyes if he did not leave. 'Be off with you, scabby scoundrel,' shouted he. And so it was that Sir Cleges opened the basket so that the chamberlain might see the gift he had brought. And when the greedy servant looked inside, his eyes lit up – miraculous midwinter cherries, fresh-grown in the middle of a cruel and hard winter at that! And so he thought to himself, 'For such a wondrous gift, the king is sure to reward this old beggar with an equally wonderful prize,' and being a covetous man, he wanted his share. He would let the old beggar pass through the gate, but only if he agreed to give the chamberlain one third of any reward that King Uther gave unto him.

Well, Sir Cleges agreed, even though that meant that he would get nothing of any reward that the king offered, for the constable, steward and chamberlain would take it all, one third each. But being a noble man, he kept his temper and continued into the great hall where Uther sat upon a fair and fine throne. Well, know, my friends, that even King Uther did not recognise his old friend now knelt before him, although unlike his greedy servants he showed the ancient stranger great kindness, especially when he opened the basket so that the king could see the gift he had brought. Uther was both astonished and delighted by what he saw – miraculous midwinter cherries, fresh-grown in the middle of a cruel and hard winter at that! The king bade the old man ask whatever he would, whatever the beggar wanted he would have as a reward.

Well my friends, what say you? What should Sir Cleges ask for? Not an easy question when you consider that he must give all the reward away. But remember what I told you at the start of this story, the old knight was a wise as well as a generous man and know I spoke true, for this is what he said: 'My Lord, I ask only that you grant me twelve blows with this, my own staff!'

Uther did not want to grant such a strange reward, but he had no choice. And true to his word Sir Cleges shared the blows out amongst his greedy enemies; the constable, the steward and the chamberlain – four whopping whacks each!

There the story ends, except to say that Uther was watching and finally recognised his old friend Sir Cleges. Seeing how the old knight had taught his servants a valuable lesson, the king gave him many rich gifts to share with his family and vassals.

The cherries were fair and so knocked from the trees,
The king's servants were foul and so knocked to their knees.

2

Gluttony

Although William the Conqueror became King of England in 1066, he spent much of his time back in Normandy where he enjoyed hunting and eating all that he caught. But the king grew so large that when in 1087 his horse tripped on rough ground, William's big belly struck the pommel of his saddle and he died a slow and painful death. So swollen had his stomach become that the dead king was too big to fit in his coffin and his belly burst open as he was squeezed inside! His son, King Henry I, is also said to have died from eating too many lampreys, long snake-like fish that were common in rivers long ago. Two kings then, father and son, who both died because of their gluttonous ways.

Gluttony *means to eat until you are full, but then to eat some more, and was thought to be a sin because gluttonous people kept all their food for themselves instead of sharing it with the poor. Medieval people believed that gluttons were selfish, only thinking of themselves.*

Of Birds and the Brothers Three

Medieval folk knew death well enough. They called him King Death, because he ruled over all, even rich and powerful men… For once long ago a king of England lay dying, but his would not be an easy death, for the king had three sons and he could not decide who among them would rule when he was dead and gone. And so it was that he desired to know something of their natures, to find out what made them the way they were. And so it was that he decided to ask each in turn this question: If you were a bird, what bird would you be and why?

The old king first sent for his eldest son, Robert, and asked him, 'If you were a bird, what bird would you be and why?' Without hesitation, the young man replied, 'I would be a falcon, for the falcon fixes its eye upon its prey, it swoops and takes all that it hunts, just as a good king should take all that he desires!'

Having heard his words, the old king sent for his second son, William Rufus, which meant William the Red, for the young man was known for his fiery hair and fiery temper. He asked the lad, 'If you were a bird, what bird would you be and why?' Without hesitation, Rufus replied, 'I would be an eagle, for the eagle is feared by all other birds, just as a good king should be feared by his people!'

Having heard his words, the old king sent for his youngest son, Henry, and asked, 'If you were a bird, what bird would you be and why?' But the boy could not decide and so went away awhile to ponder upon the riddle. And when at last he returned to his father's bedside he said, 'I would be a starling or perhaps a swan.' The king asked him to explain. 'I would be a starling,' says he, 'because it is a communal bird that lives with all the other starlings,

just as a good king should be as one with his people. And I would be a swan because it has a long neck, so that any words it speaks take a long time to travel to its beak, giving the bird time to think about all that it says, just as a good king should think long upon all that he says and all that he does.'

Well, having heard all three son's answers, the old king chose his successor. But who would you choose, my friends? I suspect many of you would favour young Henry, as would I, but alas their father was not as wise as all of you. For the old king was William I, a cruel ruler who chose his second son, William Rufus. And know that Rufus was true to his word, for when his father died, he ruled like an eagle and was feared by most of his people.

He made forest laws that prevented the poor peasants from hunting the woods and grasslands for deer, hare and boar, for such was the new king's gluttony that he wished to keep all of the animals for his own.

Such was the hatred for Rufus that his few friends warned him to be on his guard, yet the young king did not listen to any of them and not even to what was going on inside his own head. For each and every night King William Rufus was haunted by nightmares! Once, on the eve of a hunt in the New Forest, the young king dreamt that he was being bled by his surgeon. He had cut a small vein in the king's arm to let a little blood drip, drip, drip into a bowl held beneath for that purpose. But in William's dire dream, the blood would not stop dripping – instead it filled the bowl, spilling over the edge until there was so much blood it blotted out the setting sun. The king woke with a start, and ordered that his men hold candles aloft while he slept.

But the following morning the sun was shining and William Rufus was happy again, for the gluttonous monarch loved nothing more than hunting meat for his table. Better still, the king's fletcher, the man who made his arrows, presented William with a quiver of the finest arrows, each with peacock feather fletchings and all the king's friends admired them, going 'ooh' and 'ahh' many times. But Rufus wasn't about to share them with everyone; instead he gave half to his best friend, Walter Tyrel, the best bowman in the whole of England in a time before Robin Hood.

And so it was that the king and his men went hunting, but not one deer, hare or boar broke cover, not a single creature was killed. Over the course of the day, the hunting party spread out across the forest and William Rufus and his friend, Walter, found themselves alone, looking down a long track that ran west towards the setting sun. The two friends decided that it was a perfect place to wait for their prey, be it deer, hare or boar, and they hid among the ferns, one man on either side of the track. Suddenly they heard a crashing and a thrashing as a great white stag broke cover and ran between them, sprinting west towards the setting sun. Quickly Rufus loosed an arrow at the blundering beast, but it merely glanced off the stag's tough hide, the creature's sturdy skin. 'Shoot!' cried the king to Walter. 'Shoot now!' cried he, as the young man loosed his own arrow. It whirred, hissed and hummed through the air, striking its target, finding its mark, yet the animal kept running. For the fair and fine arrow, fletched

with peacock feathers, had struck William Rufus in the chest and now he lay dying.

Walter Tyrel claimed it was an accident, yet still he sailed to France, never to return. And such was the hatred for Rufus that his body was left to moulder in the woods for many days until three charcoal burners took it to Winchester, where it was buried without prayer or care. William's younger brother, Henry, became the next monarch of England, a good king who was true to his word, for like the swan and the starling he was thoughtful and as one with his people. Although, know that there were some who whispered it was he who had paid Walter Tyrel to kill his older brother. Others spoke differently. They said that it was the spirits of the woodland, the Green Man and Hern the Hunter who shot Rufus dead as revenge for his cruel forest laws and as a blood sacrifice to ensure that the woodlands of England remained forever green…

The king like the eagle wished to be feared,
So when he was shot, nobody cared.

Of the Cow that Came Home

Most medieval people believed in Heaven and Hell and would do anything they could to get close to God… For there was once a greedy priest who took much from the people of his village; from the milk their cows gave to the eggs their hens laid. Every Sunday he would preach to the poor peasants about the glories of giving, saying, 'All who give generously to my church will be rewarded with twice as much in Heaven.'

Well, this day a poor husband and wife were listening. Thinking about the rewards that were waiting for them in Heaven made them both happy and so they decided to give the priest their cow. The husband took the old beast – called old Maudy – to the priest, saying, 'If you pat her back when she is milked, Maudy will fill a bucket each day with delicious creamy milk that makes the choicest of cheese.' The priest took the cow, caring little that the poor husband and wife would go hungry without her milk, thinking only of his own bulbous belly instead. He ordered his servant to take Maudy to the barn and tie her to his own cow called Brownie, so the two could get to know each other.

But know, my friends, that Maudy did not like Brownie, for the priest's cow tugged hard at the rope that joined them, jerking her head to feed on hay and whipping old Maudy with her tail. And so it was that Maudy pulled harder still upon the rope that joined them, dragging Brownie out of the barn, past forest, field and fen, and along the track that led to the poor husband and wife's hovel, the tumbledown cottage they called home.

Well, when in the morning the poor couple found the two cows tied together, they wept

wonderful tears of joy. The priest had been right all along; those who gave generously to the church were rewarded with twice as much. For where once they had one cow, now they had two, and they hadn't even had to die and go to Heaven to get them!

The priest preached of charity, yet his own greed was great,
The poor couple who gave, replaced four hooves with eight.

Of the Friar and the Fart

Medieval friars took a vow of poverty, meaning they had no possessions. They relied on the charity of others, although not everyone was willing to give... For once there was a friar who was as big in the middle as he was tall. He was supposed to follow God in Heaven, but he much preferred to follow his belly! He travelled the highways and byways, preaching and praying to the people, warning them of the dangers of sin, while begging for food to fill his ever-growing stomach. And many poor peasants gave the friar what he asked, for in return he promised to pray for them so that they would go to Heaven when they died. 'Perhaps a small cut of cheese, or even some brawn would be good,' said the friar to each poor peasant he met, 'although beef would be finer and cake fairer still.' But in return for the poor people's generous gifts, he gave nothing but fairytales and fables, for never once did he help those who had helped him.

And so it was that the false friar continued his cheating ways, until one day he went to the home of an old man who had looked after him well enough in times past, but now the old man was very sick and for many months he had lain upon his bed. He had become but bones and blisters, sores and sorrows, for his was now a life of pain. The foul friar entered the old man's chamber and greeted him warmly, reminding the frail fellow of how generous he had been in times past. And know, my friends, that the friar was not yet finished with the old man, for gluttony was the least of his weaknesses; he was also greedy for gold! Knowing that the old man was dying, the friar wanted all of his coin for himself and his brother friars, twelve men who were also gluttonous and greedy. 'A gold coin split many ways buys very little,' says he, 'far better to give it all to me and my twelve brother friars so that we can spend it wisely, while also helping you get to Heaven.'

But the old man had had enough of the friar's greed and so begged him to come close. 'I have but one thing left to give,' said the old fellow, 'a thing so truly precious to me that I keep it hidden in this very bed.' The faithless friar wanted whatever it was, but before the old man would him let him take the gift, he made the friar promise that he would share it equally with his twelve fellow friars. Thinking it was a rich reward, perhaps even a big bag of gold, the friar knelt by the old man's bedside and swore upon Heaven and Hell that he would do exactly as the old man asked. 'By my very faith in God,' says he, 'I will share the gift with all my brothers.' And so it was that the old man told the friar to reach under his bedcovers, deep down beneath the sheets. 'Stretch out your hand, good friar,' said he, 'for the gift is just beneath my buttocks where I keep it safe from thieves.'

Now I bet some of you are thinking, 'Oh, that's a bit odd,' and you'd be right. For when the old man felt the friar's greedy, grasping hand between the crack of his cheeks, he let rip a ripe fart right into the friar's open palm! A foul and thunderous fart that found its way up the friar's sleeve, making his gown billow like whiffy washing in a wild wind!

Well, the furious friar leapt to his feet and so loud were his screams that the old man's servants cast him from the house, while the old man laughed so much that he forgot all his sores and sorrows, for a while anyway. The foul-tempered friar ran to the house of the lord of the manor, the man in charge of the medieval village. Through gritted, grinding teeth he told the nobleman of the old man's promise of the precious gift that was but a foul and thunderous fart that found its way up his sleeve, making his gown billow like whiffy washing in a wild wind! So too he told the lord of his promise to the old man, his sworn oath, that he would share the fetid fart with the twelve other friars, or risk the horrors of Hell!

Well, the lord sat quietly, for he had never seen anyone as angry as this, let alone a friar who was supposed to be so godly and good. And what could he say – for how could the moaning man share a fart with his fellow friars? 'It cannot be done,' says the lord, 'for a gusty gas cannot be divided. Far better to forget the fart and enjoy a merry meal with me.' And so it was that the friar began to eat and as his big belly grew bigger still, his anger, slowly it grew small. But one of the lord's servants had also heard the fuming friar's story, of the precious gift that was but a foul and thunderous fart that found its way up the friar's sleeve, making his gown billow like whiffy washing in a wild wind! The tale pleased him greatly, for the old man who had tricked the greedy friar was his good friend and he too wanted to play his part in the fun. And so it was that he told his lord that he had an idea how to divide the fart between the other twelve men of God and so save the fuming friar from Hell.

The clever servant told his lord that a cartwheel with twelve spokes should be brought to the hall, along with the twelve other friars and the old man who had played the putrid prank. 'Then,' says the servant, 'you must ask that the twelve friars set their noses around the rim of the cart wheel, each at the end of a spoke, while our fat friar already here squats beneath the wheel with his nose to the hub, the very centre of the wheel.' The servant also told his lord that the old man should enjoy a massive meal and not stop eating until his belly became tight and stretched like a drum. 'And then,' said the servant, 'the old fellow must be lifted on to the top of the wheel, so that he is squatting above the hub where he must let another thunderous fart. For I believe that both noise and stench will travel down each spoke and so be fairly shared between each man of God, while the false friar beneath shall have the first and foulest helping of the fart. For he is always telling us poor folk to give generously and so it's only fair that he gets the most!'

Know, my friends, that the lord laughed long, loud and lustily at the joke, but the friar did not. Instead he left the village, vowing never to return.

The friar warned all of the horrors of Hell,
But all he got in return was a handful of
smell.

3

Lust

In the year 1100, Henry, the son of William the Conqueror, became King of England and is said to have been a good ruler who helped bring Anglo-Saxons and Normans closer together. But he also had a reputation for being a lusty lad who loved ladies a lot. For although he was married to a Saxon princess called Matilda and they had a son and a daughter, he also had another twenty-five children by many other women! That's twenty-seven children in all and makes King Henry I a perfect example of lust long ago.

Lust *means to desire another person and in medieval times lustful people were thought to be much like gluttons, selfish folk who thought only of their own needs, even if it got themselves and others into trouble.*

Of the Queen's Clever Question

The noblemen and women of medieval times enjoyed epic romances about damsels in distress, while the poorer folk went for shorter, simpler tales that were often both comic and wise. What follows is a mixture of both... For once long ago there was a kind and gentle queen and Guinevere was her name. Know, my friends, that she was as fair as a May morning and although she was married to King Arthur, still many other men desired her, including a cruel man called Maleagant, who lived in a land far away. Some said he was a wizard, who wore dark magic about him as you or I might wear a coat. Some claimed he was a lord of the fairy realm, not a man, but born of the elves. While others whispered that the sun never shone upon his land, that it was a dim, dull, unhappy place where only misery grew from the cold, dead earth. Whatever the truth of it, Maleagant wanted Guinevere and so he stole her away.

King Arthur's anger at the loss of his loving wife quickly became a rampaging rage and he rode forth with his most trusted warriors – knights like Sir Kay and Authur's own brave nephew, Gawain, made up his mighty war band. They rode out over high fell and low dale, galloping without caution between gnarled and knotted trees, only slowing when they had need to cut their way through the cruel and twisted thorns that grew beyond. On and on they rode, sleeping beneath snow-leaden skies with only their armour for shelter, while crows perched upon the bare black branches above and piped piteously as Arthur and his knights passed by.

On and on they rode, passing a lake that was as black as blood upon a moonless night, until at last they came to Maleagant's castle, set high on the rocky cliff face. King Arthur drew his mighty magic sword, Excalibur, and challenged the cruel lord to a fight, calling out, 'You have taken my wife so now I shall take your life, if you are brave enough to fight me, man to man.'

But Maleagant laughed, for like many a cruel man he was a coward who sent out one of his knights instead. A wild warrior strode forth from his lord's fortress, wielding a wicked weapon, a sword as tall as a man and now he and Arthur did battle. Their swords clashed and their shields smashed together throughout the night and into the following day, while their armour glistened with each other's blood.

Maleagant had hoped for an easy victory, but saw that even his biggest and best knight could not get the better of Arthur. Fearing further bloodshed and perhaps even the loss of his own life, Maleagant brought forth Guinevere and begged for her help, hoping that she would speak kind and thoughtful words. The queen stepped forward and this

is what she said: 'Since my husband and his enemy have fought so hard to have me for a wife, then have me both shall. For one will be my husband while the leaves lie heavy upon the trees and the other when they do not.'

Well, quickly Maleagant claimed Guinevere in that time when the trees were bare, for he could think only of winter, the dark cold months when the leaves have fallen and he could keep warm with the queen beneath the sheets of his bed. But he spoke in haste, for Maleagant forgot that there are some trees like the holly, and others covered in ivy, that never lose their leaves, staying green throughout the year. And so it was that he lost what he desired most, for Guinevere went back to her husband, King Arthur, and was happy once more to be his loving wife. Although know, my friends, that if you seek out other Arthurian legends, you'll see that the king and queen were not always as happy as in the tale told here.

The cruel lord's choice was guided by lust,
And so quick his reply, his desires became dust.

Of the Cook and the Crane

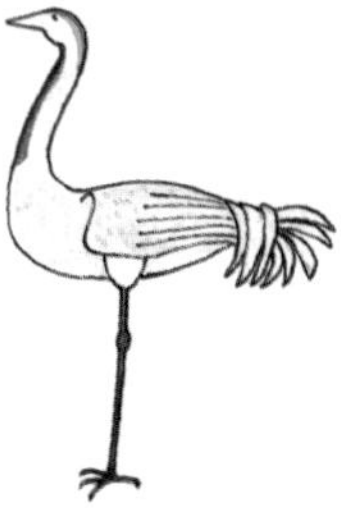

Lust means one person's desire for another, although this story starts with a lord who loved his pet falcon most of all... For once there was a nobleman who spent his days hunting, riding out on horseback with bow or sharpened spear and with his favourite bird of prey, his beloved gyrfalcon, upon his arm. The bird took pigeons from the air, also ducks and geese, but this day it swooped down upon a crane, a long-legged, long-necked bird with a beak that was as sharp as any of the lord's own spears. But this bird's beak was used for spearing fish and was no use against the fierce falcon, and so it was that the crane was killed and the nobleman sent it to his cook, looking forward to the fine feast to come.

The nobleman's old cook was master of his craft and soon had the bird plucked and prepared for the spit that turned in front of the fire. Before long the crane was roasting to perfection as the clever cook basted the tender bird in its own juices, spooning them over its crisp, cooking flesh that smelt as good as it looked. But if the capable cook had one fault, it was that he lusted after one of the lord's servants, a young woman who cleaned and cared for his clothes. For she had a soft singsong voice that warmed the cook's heart and a smile in her eye that made his head spin. The young woman came into the kitchen where the crane was still roasting. Its sweet-smelling flesh reached her nose and she begged the cook for just a small taste. But the cook would not give in to her desires, for he was worried what his lord would do if his cooked crane was not complete. The young woman grew angry, stomping her feet, saying, 'Well, if you won't give me what I want this day, you shall

get nothing from me, not even a sweet kiss goodnight.' The cook knew her meaning, that they would never be together, and although he feared his noble lord, he was even more scared of losing her. And so it was that he cut one of the legs off the roasting crane and gave it to his true love.

Well, that night the roast crane was brought before the lord and his many important guests, but when he saw a leg was missing, the lord chided his chef, roaring rude words at him and demanding the cook tell him where it had gone. 'Why, my Lord,' said the clever chef, 'what do you mean? For everyone knows that cranes only have one leg, while other birds have two.' The lord grew angrier still and threatened to beat the cook if he could not prove what he said was true. And so the following day the lord, his guests and the cook rode out towards the river where at last they found a flock of cranes all standing on one leg, as they so often do when they are fast asleep. Now, you might think the cunning cook was in the clear, but he was not, for his lord galloped into the river, shouting, 'HO! HO!' and 'HAAA!', waking the cranes, who in their alarm put down their other legs and took flight. 'Nice try, cook,' says the lord, 'but as you see cranes have two legs and so prepare to be beaten until your bones break!'

But the clever chef cooked up another idea, for this is what he said: 'Why, my Lord, you were right after all, cranes do have two legs and not just one. But,' said he, 'you didn't shout out "HO! HO!" and "HAAA!" last night at the feast. If you had, the cooked crane would have put its other leg down and flown away!'

Know, my friends, that the lord laughed long, loud and lustily and all was forgiven. The cook and the servant were married and they shared many a roasted crane, always one leg each.

The crane's stolen leg was fine in the eating,
While the cook's clever words prevented a beating.

Of the Fake Flood

At medieval universities young men were taught astrology, how the movement of the stars affected people on earth, nowadays seen by many as silly nonsense, but taken very seriously long ago… For once there were three men who were oh so very different to each other. The first and oldest was a carpenter called John, whose skills working wood were much admired, but his crafty hands were not matched by the workings of his head. It was like a dark and empty place where the candles had been snuffed out long ago.

The second was a clerk called Absolon, a bookkeeper is what we might call him today. He cared only for his outward appearance;

bright colours, fine laces and frills were his passion, he was like a peacock in human form.

The third was a student called Nicolas, a clever young man well-schooled in alchemy and astrology, the study of chemistry and the stars up above. But for all his wisdom, he was a lad led by desire! For the student lived with the old carpenter and when not studying the heavens above he would be studying the old carpenter's young wife, Alison, for she was the only thing the three men had in common. All loved her, even Absolon, for even a peacock must find a mate once in a while.

All adored Alison, but Nicolas lusted after her and she lusted after him. Her husband, old John, paid her little attention and so Alison had fallen for the young student's clever talk and the sweet melodies he played upon a harp. And now the lonely young woman and Nicolas wanted to play together!

And so it was that they made a plan – that he would take no food offered by the carpenter's servants and that she would sneak him food late at night when all were in bed.

And that she would tell her husband that he had not left his room for a week. Well, my friends, know that Alison played her part to perfection, telling the old carpenter that Nicolas had eaten nothing but the stale air of his room and drank nothing but his own bitter tears for many days. 'For all I hear,' says she to her husband, 'are the young student's sobs as I pass close by his room.'

Well, old John feared that the student was struck down with some deadly disease or, even worse, that all that book learning had gone to his head. Remember, my friends, that this was medieval times when few could read and the old man thought that no good would come of prying too deep into God's mysterious ways. He went to the student's room and, peering through a small hole in the door, the carpenter saw the clever lad sitting bolt upright at the end of his bed, mouth agape – moonstruck he was. And so the old man wasted no time lifting the door off its hinges and taking hold of Nicolas, shaking him by his shoulders. The student began to sob loudly. 'Alas!' cried he. 'Woe!' cried he. 'Alas and woe, that the world must come to an end so soon.' And now the lying lad told old John that his study of the stars had brought bad news; that the world was going to end next Monday night at nine of the clock. For at that time there would be a great flood and everyone would be drowned!

Nicolas sobbed some more, so too old John – the louder the cries of the one, the louder the reply of the other. For the old man feared for his life, so too his young wife, and he begged the student for words of comfort. 'Is there nothing that can be done?' pled he. The slightest of smiles passed across the clever lad's lips, for the plan was working. He told the old carpenter that he must fill three barrels with food and drink and haul them up high into the rafters of the house. 'And then,' said the student, 'when the flood comes we can climb one into each and float away, so escaping mankind's doom!'

Well, John's love of life was only matched by his stupidity and all the next day he heaved, humped and hefted three heavy barrels stocked with food and drink into the rafters. And that night the old man, his young wife and the student climbed one into each, there to await the great deluge, the mock medieval flood! And so it was that all three sat quietly, but only one was sleepy. For while John filled his belly with beer and listened fitfully for

raindrops upon the roof, Alison and Nicolas were wide awake, listening for the old man's snores. And when at last he fell asleep they shot down the ladders like ferrets down a coney hole and went to her chamber, where they climbed beneath the blankets and kissed and cuddled close!

But even peacocks must find a mate once in a while and it just so happened to be this night when Absolon the clerk came a-wooing at Alison's window. There he stood in his fine laces and frills and called out, 'Awake my peach, my pretty chick. Awake my lambkin and kiss me now.' But Alison had waited far too long to be with Nicolas and so she swore at Absolon, saying, 'Get ye gone' and 'Tarry here no more.' But the lovelorn peacock would not leave unless she gave him a kiss. 'Just one kiss,' says he, 'is all I desire.' But Alison had other ideas. 'One kiss, eh?' says she. 'Well close your eyes, clerk, and pucker up!' The young woman rose from her bed and in the dark she did open the window and stuck out her bare backside! Her buttocks went one way while Absolon's lips went the other and he did kiss her right on her naked bum!

Well, the clerk was a finicky and fussy fellow who knew right away what was wrong. The picky peacock spat and scrubbed at his lips with straw and cloth while Alison and Nicolas laughed until they sobbed. Angered by her trickery, Absolon went to see a blacksmith going early about his business, hammering heated iron into knives, nails and more. He begged the blacksmith give him a red-hot rod of iron from the fiery furnace, which quickly he carried back to the fair young woman's window and there Absolon begged another kiss from Alison to say sorry for the cruel trick she had played. 'Just one more kiss,' called he, 'and I will bother you no more.'

Well know, my friends, that Nicolas had risen from the warm bed to pee and having filled a nearby pot right to the brim he wanted his share of the fun. The cunning lad crept to the window and in a high voice, more like Alison's than his own, he called out, 'Get

ready my sweetheart, for here I come,' as he did stick out his brawny and bristly backside! And a handsome piece of work it was, made all the more impressive for that he let rip a thunderclap of a fart! The student's booming buttocks went one way, the clerk's red-hot rod of iron the other, as Absolon did smite Nicolas upon the bare bum!

'ARRGH!' screamed the student and 'OOOOW!' screamed he, as he leapt thither and yon about the room, rubbing his reddened rear. Now I don't know about you, my friends, but if I were burnt on me behind, I'd want to cool me charred cheeks quickly and so did Nicolas. 'WATER!' yelled he, 'I MUST HAVE WATER NOW!' So loud were the student's screams that they woke old John, up high in his barrel above. Roused from his sleep and hearing the loud lad's shouts for water, the old man thought the flood had come and now he must go. With sharpened axe he cut the ropes and all three barrels, meat, ale and old carpenter came crashing down, not stopping until they met the cellar floor.

There were once three men who were oh so very different to each other. The first was an old carpenter called John, whose skills working wood were much admired, but now his arm was broken and others mocked him much behind his back.

The second, a clerk called Absolon, cared only for his outward appearance; bright colours, fine laces and frills were his passion, but he could never get the wicked whiff from under his nose.

The third, a clever student called Nicolas, was well-schooled in alchemy and astronomy, but from that day forward he did all his studying standing up.

While one man did yell, the second he fell,
And the third could never get rid of that smell.

4

Sloth

In 1192 ,King Richard I of England was captured while returning from the Crusades. He was handed over to the Holy Roman Emperor, Henry VI, who ransomed him, meaning he would not let Richard go until he was paid 100,000 pounds of silver, a fortune long ago. The poor people of England had to pay high taxes to help raise the ransom money and yet still Richard was called the Lionheart and celebrated as a good and powerful ruler. But the truth is that he was a very lazy king when it came to ruling England. In the ten years that Richard reigned, he only spent about six months in this country, preferring to live in France instead. He used England to pay for his battles and crusades in other lands while leaving his foolish younger brother, Prince John, in charge, which makes King Richard I a perfect example of sloth.

Sloth *meant being lazy in medieval times. A slothful person was someone who didn't help other people, not caring when others were wronged.*

Of a Lesson Learnt

Some of the kings of medieval England were hated by those they ruled, yet in stories at least, some monarchs ruled well… For there was once a wise king who hoped his son would be much wiser still. And so it was that he had the best tutors in the land teach the prince of the movement of the stars in the heavens, of the many languages of man, of the history of his own country and of which countries went where in the world.

The prince worked hard at his lessons, for he was no lazy lad. Until one day his father decided it was time to test the boy's wit and wisdom, to see if he was ready to rule. He offered his son a great bag of gold, telling the lad that he could spend it however he liked.

'Build a great palace if you will,' said the king. 'Buy fair and fine clothes, or even give it away if that pleases you most.'

The prince took the coin, while the king ordered the boy's tutors to follow him, so all would know whether or not the money was well spent. But the learned men had a long wait, for the prince was in no hurry to get rid of the gold. Until one day the young man stood watching from the palace, looking down at all the people going about their business. Some strode past in magnificent gowns of fine cloth that stretched across their well-fed flesh, while others limped by dressed only in coarse rags that barely covered their thin, scrawny bodies, and now the prince began to wonder about the people who lived in his father's land.

And so it was that he ordered his teachers to fetch some of the people to him, so that he might know more of where they came from and what they did. Soon a large crowd of people stood before the prince and there was one among them who caught the boy's eye,

for he was dressed in fine robes and stared back at the prince, never once looking away. 'Tell me,' said the prince, 'where are you from and why are you here in my city?' The man in fine robes smiled, for he had nothing to hide. 'I am a merchant,' replied he, 'who buys and sells at the market. And all that I have is from my own hard work, for my father and mother were poor, but now I am rich.'

The prince looked to another man dressed much more poorly than the first. 'Tell me,' said the prince, 'where are you from and why are you here in my city?' The man did not smile, for it seemed he had much to hide. Yet the son of the king had asked him a question and so he had no choice but to reply. 'I once ruled a far-off land,' said he, 'but I was an idle, lazy king, a bad monarch who only looked after himself. And so my people stripped me of my crown and riches and drove me from my realm.'

Having heard both men's words, the prince decided to give all his father's gold to one of these two men. But which one should he give the coin to? The merchant who had worked hard all his life, or to the lazy king who thought only of himself? I bet many of you would give the gold to the merchant, as a prize for all his hard work. But know, my friends, that he gave it to the idle ruler who had only done his people wrong. 'Why?' I hear you asking, which is something the prince's father also wanted to know. He asked his son to explain his choice, saying, 'Why have you wasted my gold on a man who was brought low by his own laziness?' The prince, though, had an answer. 'You are wrong, Father, your gold was not wasted,' replied he. 'I gave it to the poor man as a reward, for it was he who taught me what happens to bad kings who do not care for their people. And while I have learnt many wondrous things from my tutors, from the movement of the stars in the heavens to the many languages of man, none has been so valuable a lesson as this lazy man has taught me this day.'

The king was well pleased with the prince's wise words and willingly gave up his throne to the lad. And as his father had hoped, the young man became a hard-working monarch who ruled the land well.

The king gave gold to test his son's right to rule,
The son spent it wisely, for he was no fool.

Of the Rascal and the Rug

Here sits a tale about a trickster, one of many you'll find in this book. But this knave and rapscallion from Germany was the master of fleecing foolish folk… For once long ago there was a beguiler of the foolish; a coney-catching cunning man called Till Eulenspiegel, who travelled from town to town, village to village, and house to house, wearing many different disguises. Sometimes a priest, sometimes a potter, and sometimes a pedlar of wares, but this day he arrived in a city disguised as a scholar, an educated man in medieval times.

Till went about the place claiming that he was the most learned man in the land, a master of alchemy and astrology and that none could challenge his wit. And so it was that his boasts reached the ears of the chancellor, the man in charge of the city's university, where all the wisest men did dwell. He was a clever fellow who did not like our trickster's bragging ways. And so it was that he sent a messenger to tell Till Eulenspiegel of a test. 'If you can answer three questions, the chancellor will reward you with a hundred gold coins,' said he. 'But if you cannot answer all three, you will be whipped through the streets of this city.'

Know, my friends, that a lesser trickster would have fled, but not our roguish rascal. The following day Till arrived at the university wearing his student's cap and gown, bowing low to the chancellor and all the other scholars gathered there. The chancellor asked his first question. 'Tell me if you can,' said he, 'what am I thinking?' Our cunning conman smiled broadly, for the answer was easy. 'You are thinking that you are wiser than me,' replied he. The scholars all laughed, although the chancellor did not, for Till spoke true. He could not argue with that.

The chancellor asked his second question. 'Tell me if you can,' said he, 'how many hairs are there in my beard?' Our cunning conman smiled broadly, for the answer was easy. He stepped forward and, plucking a hair from the old man's chubby chin, he said, 'There is one less than there was a moment ago!' The scholars all laughed although the chancellor did not, for Till spoke true. He could not argue with that.

The chancellor asked his third question. 'Tell me if you can,' said he, 'how many stars are there in the sky?' Our cunning conman smiled broadly, for the answer was easy. He pointed to a bearskin that lay in front of the chancellor's throne and said, 'There are the same number of stars in the heavens as there are hairs on this rug!' This time the scholars did not laugh, for the chancellor leapt angrily from his seat, roaring rude words at Till, for how could he possibly know that?

For the first time our roguish knave looked fearful, perhaps pondering upon the chancellor's wicked whip. But then he smiled broadly once more. 'My Lord, I was wrong,' says Till, 'for I forgot that I saw a shooting star last night falling from the sky.' And stepping forward he plucked another hair, although this time from the bearskin rug. 'Now,' said he, 'there are the same number of stars in the heavens as there are hairs on this rug!' The scholars all laughed although the chancellor did not, for know, my friends, that he was a lazy man, too slothful to count the hairs on the bearskin, or the stars in the sky. And so it was that Till Eulenspiegel continued on his journey, although now he was weighed down by a hundred gold coins.

The trickster was clever, a credit to his trade,
The chancellor was idle and for that he paid.

Of the Man with the Braying Backside

If you were unwell in medieval times a doctor might purge you of your sickness by giving you medicines that would make you fart and far worse... For once there was a doctor who made medicines to cure all ailments, from coughs and cankers to belly aches and burns; he could cure them all. So great was his fame that lords and ladies, merchants and mayors sought his help when they were sick and were willing to pay well for his cures. And so it was that the doctor was a rich and busy man.

But one day a poor man came to see the doctor, for he had lost his donkey and was far too lazy to look for it himself. Having heard of the doctor's clever ways with medicine the poor man decided to ask his advice. 'For after all,' thought he, 'if the doctor is sage enough to cure the sick, he must be learned enough to find that which is lost!' But when the poor man arrived at the doctor's fine house he found the man of medicine already surrounded by rich folk, all waving full purses and demanding that the dependable doctor heal them first.

The poor man pushed through the crowd and begged the clever doctor's help. But such was the din as all spoke at once that he could not hear the poor man's words and, seeing that he had little money to pay, the doctor gave him his cheapest and foulest medicine, for there were far richer people in need of his help. 'Drink it straight down and be gone,' says the doctor and even though the medicine tasted as bad as it smelt, the poor man did as he was told. For he felt certain that the clever doctor knew what he was doing.

But the ghastly green liquid was a purge to empty sick people of all that made them

ill and now the poor man's belly began to rumble, grumble and groan. He pulled down his hose, his much-mended medieval trousers, and his bum near exploded as he let rip a long, loud and lusty fart! Know, my friends, that his backside bellowed and blew hard, a rasping and roaring ripe fart that rose up at the end and sounded like the braying of a donkey.

And no sooner had the poor man finished his ferocious fart than his own lost donkey replied, also braying loudly. Thinking it was another donkey, his own animal came close, but all the donkey found was his master, the poor man, who happily took the animal home. He told everyone he met that the doctor was a very clever man indeed. For not only could he cure coughs and cankers, bellyaches and burns, but his medicines could also help find a bellowing, braying beast!

The doctor made medicines to cure the sick
and the wonky,
But they could also be used to summon a
donkey.

5

In 1215 King John was forced to seal Magna Carta, which means 'The Great Charter'. It was a list of demands written to protect the rights of the great landowners of medieval England, the nobles and barons of long ago. But John was a proud man who thought that he should be able to do as he wanted and so he asked the pope, the leader of the Church in Rome, to annul the charter, meaning to undo what had been done. Such was John's pride that he went to war with his barons, who brought over the french prince, Louis, to take the throne of England. He ran away from his barons and lost his gold and jewels in the mud of the Wash, a wide river mouth between the counties of Norfolk and Lincolnshire. Then John caught dysentery, a painful disease, and he died at Newark Castle in Nottinghamshire the same year. Well, they say that pride comes before a fall and that's certainly true of bad King John!

Pride – *to think yourself better and more deserving than other folk – was yet another sin, for medieval people believed that proud folk always put themselves first. Pride is closely related to vanity and boastfulness, and proud people often struggle to see their own faults.*

Of the Best of Blades

Medieval England was feudal, which meant that the king gave land to his noblemen in exchange for their promise to fight for him during times of war. In turn the nobles gave land to their knights, who promised to serve only them… For once there was a prince who was on a journey with one of his father's nobles, an old soldier who rode with his own knights at his back. Where they were going I cannot say, for I was not there, but as I heard tell, the road was long, the track dry and dusty, as was their talk that day.

For the prince grew bored and began to brag to the nobleman of his expensive clothes, his swift horse and finally about his newly made sword, a fine sword unmarked by war or time. The boastful boy drew the sword, the light glancing off the highly polished blade, so too the jewels that studded its hilt. 'Behold,' said the prince, 'the sword of a future king of this land,' and, flourishing both his new blade and pride in equal measure, he proclaimed it to be 'the strongest, most powerful of blades ever forged.'

But the old nobleman shook his head, saying, 'My Lord, while your sword is indeed fair, it is not the most powerful, for mine is far mightier than yours.'

Know, my friends, that the prince grew angry at the old soldier's disrespect, all the more so because he knew the man's sword was inferior to his own. For it was scarred by battle, a war-weary weapon, stained with dirt and blood. 'You lie,' said the prince, 'for your sword is base-wrought, a poorly made blade that is but a pebble from the beach in comparison to the crisp-cut diamond that is my sword!'

But still the nobleman would not agree and so the prince grew angrier still.

'Show me,' demanded the prince, 'show me if you can how your sword is stronger than my own.' And so it was that the old soldier drew his ancient battle-worn blade, holding it high for his own loyal knights to see and as he did, they all drew their swords in support of their master, thus proving his was the most mighty of swords.

The prince had done nothing, that's why he
was bored,
The soldier fought hard, as had his sword.

Of the Cock, the Crow and the Cunning Fox

Tales about tricksters were very popular in medieval times and sometimes they took the form of animals… For once in a deep, dark wood long ago an animal was walking, stalking even. It was red of fur, fleet of foot, with crafty clever eyes and wicked teeth. For it was a fox called Reynard, a beast whose belly barked loudly, for he had yet to eat this day and already the sun was lying low. So loudly that it sent the crows cawing noisily into the air, angry at having been disturbed from their evening roosts, their calls cold, cruel and some might say callous, even, although I do not.

All the crows flew away, save one, for looking up, Reynard saw an old bird who sat silently upon the bough. The crow said nowt and squinting through the gloom the hungry fox could see why – the old crow had a beak full of cheese and it was a hard cheese in more ways than one. For having but a small beak, the old crow could not chew and so it sat silently, pondering how best to devour its prize.

The piece of cheese was small, a mean feast you might say, but to a sturdy fox with a bellyful of nothing, it was a banquet for the sharing. 'Good crow,' said Reynard, 'fine crow,' said he, 'will you not fly down and share your cheese with me?' The old crow sat silently and shook its head, for having a beak full of cheese, it could not say no. 'Dear crow,' said Reynard, 'fair crow,' said he, 'if you fly down and share your meal with me, I will gladly bite the cheese in two so that you can swallow your half and I swallow mine.' But the old crow sat silently and shook its head, for having a beak full of cheese, it could not say no. 'Beloved crow,' said Reynard, 'worthy crow,' said he, 'if you share your dinner with me I should be your guardian against all who would do you wrong.' But the old crow sat silently and shook its head, for having a beak full of cheese, it could not say no.

Well, the piece of cheese was small, a meagre morsel you might say, but to a sturdy fox with a bellyful of nowt, it was a banquet for the taking and so Reynard praised the old crow's lustrous black feathers and even its coarse caw. 'There are some that say your call is cold and cruel,' said Reynard, 'some say callous even, but not I,' as now he compared the old crow's call to the gentle hum of the bees buzzing over the summer meadow and to the light, bright tinkling of the stream as it caressed the rocks beneath. 'Whenever I hear you caw,' said the hungry fox, 'it freshens my weary mind, so caw for me good crow,' said he, 'nay – sing out for me long, loud and lustily this night.'

Something stirred in the old crow's vain heart. Never before had it been so praised. Yes, it knew its feathers were beautiful, all crows do, but its caw? The old crow had always thought it cold, cruel, callous even. And so it was that the bird went, 'CAAAAW!' And as it did that small piece of cheese fell from the old crow's beak and into the mouth of Reynard waiting patiently below!

Well, Reynard ate that night, but a morsel of cheese won't go far and so he thought now of feasting upon chicken… For once there lived an old woman who had herself a small yard wherein she kept seven hens who were seven sisters and the seven wives of her strutting cockerel, Chanticleer. His feathers were a rich silky black in colour, much like a king's finest gown, and his coxcomb, the crown upon his head, was redder than the reddest ruby ever dug from the earth. He was a fair and fine cockerel, although he knew his worth and was as vain as he was handsome; he especially loved his crow. Not a crow like the bird who lost its cheese, you understand, oh no, for by crow I mean his call. His crow was mellower than the mellow organ that could be heard sweetly playing in the church every Sunday. For he went, 'COCK-A-DOODLE-DOOOOOOO!'

The seven hens who were seven sisters loved Chanticleer, but one was devoted to him more than the others. Her name was Pertelote, a pretty hen, and they would sing together, she gently clucking and he crowing loudly. But all was not well with Chanticleer, for his sleep was haunted by nightmares. In the early hours when night was near finished, but day had yet to begin, the cockerel would moan and groan and this morning Pertelote asked him what ailed him, what brought him so low?

The cockerel told her how he dreamt that he was being watched by a cruel creature. 'It was red of fur and fleet of foot,' said he, 'with crafty clever eyes and wicked teeth.' But Pertelote cared little for bad dreams or their meanings; she thought that nightmares were caused by overeating. 'Dreams,' said she, 'come from having bad wind in your belly.' And she told the concerned cockerel that all he need do was let out a long fart and all would be well!

Chanticleer wasn't so sure, for he believed that bad dreams were portents, meaning warnings of many a misfortune to come. Yet now the sun was coming up and Pertelote began to speak of pleasant things, clucking softly, and the cockerel forgot all his woes and worries as once more he became the boastful bird of old. He strutted proudly amongst his hens, like a king from a far-off land, swaggering about his magnificent palace. And as he strutted, he went, 'COCK-A-DOODLE-DOOOOOOO!'

The careless cockerel forgot all about his bad dream, a mistake to be sure, for Reynard had slipped through the hedges and lay low close by. Chanticleer flounced and flew up onto the fence, desiring to show himself off to the rest of the farm as he made ready to crow. But then he caught sight of the fearsome fox and in his panic he would have surely fled had it not been for the cruel creature's sly and silver tongue. 'Good cockerel,' said Reynard, 'fine cockerel,' said he, 'do not be afraid of me. For I have only crept close to hear you sing.'

And now he compared the vain cockerel's crow to the gentle hum of the bees buzzing over the summer meadow and to the light, bright tinkling of the stream as it caressed the rocks beneath. For it had worked well enough upon the old crow with the cheese! 'Whenever I hear you crow,' says Reynard, 'it freshens my weary mind, so crow for me, good cockerel,' says he, 'nay – sing out long, loud and lustily this day.' Well, the old crow had been vain, but know that the cockerel was cockier still – he puffed out his chest and went, 'COCK-A—'

But before the cockerel could doodle his doo Reynard grabbed him by the throat and, casting the proud bird over his shoulder, ran back towards the woods. Yet the evil deed was seen by all the hens in the yard and all began to screech and squawk as the old woman came running. So too, men working in the fields nearby, all of them chasing Reynard the fox. But the cunning creature was already far away and it looked as if Chanticleer would make a mightier morsel than the cheese!

But it is worth remembering, my friends, that pride is a weakness found in many creatures, for Reynard knew he was cunning and clever and it was this very fact that gave the cockerel some hope. 'Good fox,' said Chanticleer, 'fine fox,' said he, 'you have truly beaten and bested me, and also all of those who give chase.' But Reynard said nothing, for having a mouth full of cockerel he could not say yes! 'Dear fox,' said the cockerel, 'fair fox,' said he, 'if I were you, I should want them to know how cunning and clever I was. Indeed, I would shout, "Go home you stupid yokels, a plague on all of you, for now I'm almost at the woods, there is nothing you can do".' Reynard thought this a fine idea and turning to face the old woman and everyone else, he called out, 'Go home—'

But before the vain fox had barely begun his boast, Chanticleer broke free from between his terrible teeth and flew up high into a tree. And so it was that he was returned safely to the seven hens who were seven sisters and his seven wives. Although know that Chanticleer was no longer the finest crowing cockerel in the parish; for while his Cock-A-Doodle was still decent enough, his Doo had disappeared.

The cock was almost eaten, like cheese falling from the sky,
But the fox was also foolish, more vain than he was sly.

Of the Nightingale that Knew All

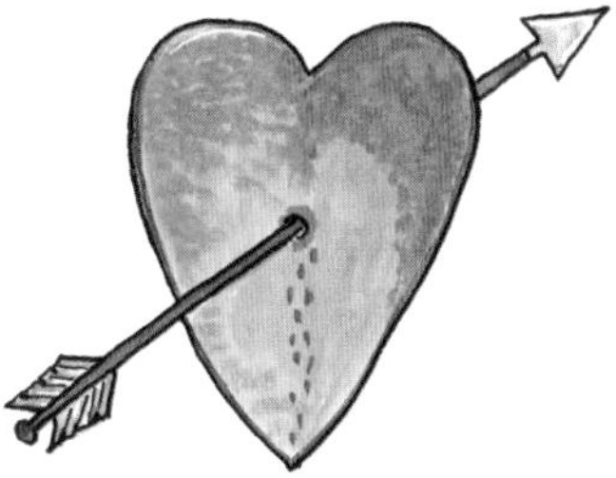

In medieval times men and women who wished to marry would 'plight their troth', meaning they would promise themselves to each other. Tokens such as rings were exchanged, although sometimes even more precious gifts were offered in an attempt to win a wife… For once there was a young man who wished to marry a gentlewoman and he lavished many gifts upon her. But none seemed to please the young woman, for she would not marry him.

One day the young man lay in the long grass of a pleasant garden pondering upon how he could win the lady's love, when he heard a nightingale singing close by. Its song was sweeter than honey and the young man knew at last how he would win the gentlewoman's love. He would give her the nightingale in a golden cage, for the bird's tender tunes were sure to melt the young woman's hard heart and make her his forever more.

And so it was that the young man set traps to capture the bird and the following day he was overjoyed to see that he had caught the nightingale in a snare, a thin cord that pulled tight about the bird's tiny and delicate leg. The terrified bird warbled and whistled, chirruped and chirped, desperate to escape as the young man came close by. He took hold of the nightingale, gripping it tight in his fist, and so it decided to beg the young man for its life. Now I know what some of you are thinking, that birds do not speak English, or any other human language come to that. But know that in medieval tales other animals like foxes and wolves could talk and since the young man did not understand the nightingale's warbles and whistles, chirrups and chirps, what other choice did it have? 'If you let me go this day,' said the brave bird to the lovelorn lad, 'I will give you three gifts far more valuable than my song, for I will give you wisdom that will help you win your lady's true love.'

The young man was as surprised as some of you that the bird could speak, which is perhaps why he agreed to let it go, although only when it had granted him the prizes it promised. 'Hear and heed my words,' said the nightingale. 'Firstly, do not believe everything you hear. Secondly, always keep a firm grasp on everything you have. And thirdly,' said the bird, 'do not cry for what you have lost.' As promised, the young man listened to the wise words and then let the nightingale go. It flew up high and began singing its song as sweet as honey, such a beautiful tune that the young man felt joyful. But his joy would be short-lived, for now the nightingale called out, 'You should not have let me go, for inside my belly is a jewel the size of a man's fist. A fine gift for your lady that would have easily won her heart.'

Hearing the bird's words, the young man grew tearful, thinking of the great jewel and the lady he had lost. He begged the bird to fly back down, hoping to trap it once more in his snares. But the nightingale would not come close, saying, 'Do you think I would listen to a fellow as foolish as you? For I gave you three pieces of wisdom, but while you listened, you did not learn from what I said. Firstly, I told you not to believe all that you hear, but still you trusted that a tiny bird like me could have a great jewel inside it as big as a man's clenched fist, when you had already held me in yours! Secondly, I told you to hold on to everything you have, yet still you let me go! And thirdly I told you not to cry over all that you have lost, but still you weep and wail now you have lost me! You are a proud man who did not truly hear or heed my words. Nor have you heard what the gentlewoman has been trying to tell you, for it was not your lavish gifts she did not want, but you who will never be hers.'

The nightingale flew high and sang many sweet songs,
The young man was vain and saw none of his wrongs.

6

Greed

So far my introductions have focused on the sins of kings, but when it comes to greed I'm not sure which medieval ruler I'd pick, for it was in the nature of kings to be greedy! Instead I'll start this chapter in 1348 when a deadly disease travelled across Europe into England. Painful swellings called buboes appeared on the sick person's body and they died in just two or three days. It was the bubonic plague, what we call the Black Death, although they also called it the Great Pestilence long ago. We now know that it was spread by fleas that were carried on rats, but back then many believed it was God, punishing the wicked for their sins, while others said it was caused by bad smells coming from the waste that piled up in medieval towns. The plague killed nearly half the people of England and Europe and so if ever a disease could be called greedy, it was this one.

Greed, *also called avarice, meant the desire to take much more than you needed. It was thought a sin because a greedy person might steal, or become a miser; a man or woman who was unwilling to share their good fortune with others.*

Of the Youths who Dealt with Death

In medieval times everyone drank ale, even young folk like you, although it often led to drunkenness and all kinds of wrongdoing... For picture if you will, my friends, a great city long ago – the crowded marketplace full of hustle and bustle, with the sound of men and women buying and selling, and of children playing with the pigs and dogs in the narrow, crowded streets. Smell the air, thick with the fair aroma of freshly baked bread and exotic herbs and spices brought from distant lands.

But now a month has passed; look again and you will see that where once all was hustle and bustle, now weeds grow between the cracked paving stones. Where once the air was filled with children's laughter, now all that can be heard is the sound of wailing and

grief. And where once there was the smell of freshly baked bread, now there is only the rotten reek of death. For the Black Death had come to the city and some hid in churches now that the pestilence was upon them, praying for their souls, while others cowered in the alehouses, drowning their sorrows and trying to forget all those they had lost.

And so my story begins with three foolish young men who were hiding in an alehouse, getting drunk on cheap ale and playing at cards and dice. All three were making merry until they were disturbed by the sad and sorrowful toll of a bell and a distant voice calling out, 'BRING OUT YOUR DEAD. BRING OUT YOUR DEAD.' And now all three watched as a body was carted past the alehouse window, on its way to be buried in a mass grave, dug to take many dead people. Well, all three desired to know who it was who had died, and the alehouse keeper told them that it was their friend who had lost his life while drinking on the very bench where they now sat. 'And as he sat there,' said the alehouse keeper, 'a softly treading thief named Death came and stole the life from him. It was Death the thief,' said he, 'who steals the life from us all. Old and young, rich and poor, all of us will be the victims of his crimes.'

The three foolish youths pondered upon the alehouse keeper's words, each thinking, 'Yes! Death is a thief who steals the life of men as if it were no more than a few coins in a poor beggar's purse. And as a thief, should he not be punished for his crimes?' The three foolish youths drank some more and, as they drank, their anger, like their foolishness, grew. Anger at the loss of their friend, anger at that ruffian Death. And so it was that all three drew their knives and brought them down into the bench where their friend had died. Each swore an oath upon his life, making an unbreakable promise that they would kill Death and so put an end to his thieving ways.

The three foolish youths set forth upon their witless quest and a crack-brained adventure it was, for they knew not what Death looked like, nor where he could be found. But they had not gone far when they met an old man with bent, twisted limbs, who greeted them warmly, saying, 'God bless and keep you gentlemen.' But their reply was less kind, for all three wondered how come a frail old fellow like he was still alive when so many young people had died of the plague. And so they asked him.

'Old man,' said they.

'Yes?' said he.

'Old man,' said they, 'how come you have not yet perished of the foul pestilence that is upon the land?' (For that is how they spoke in medieval times!)

The old man smiled sadly, telling them that he was trapped like a prisoner in his ancient body. 'My limbs ache,' said he, 'so too my heart, and often I beg Mother Earth to take me, but she won't and I am stuck here still.'

But the three foolish youths did not believe the old man; instead they thought him Death's friend, who knew where the foul thief hid. And so they asked him.

'Old man,' said they.

'Yes?' said he.

'Old man,' said they, 'it is Death we seek, so tell us now where he hides.'

The withered old man's dull eyes flashed suddenly brightly. 'So it's Death you seek is it?' said he. 'Well I'll tell you now I've seen him, yes I have. To find Death simply follow the crooked road to the oak tree yonder and there you will find him waiting!'

The three foolish youths drew their knives and ran towards the gnarled and knotted tree, but when they arrived there was no sign of Death. Instead piled high round its roots were gold coins. They rolled in them, they cast them into the air and cried, 'Woo-hoo!', for they were as rich as rich can be and you can't get much richer than that!

Well, my friends, imagine that it was you who found all that gold. What would you spend it on? Perhaps a big telly, a fast car, or maybe you'd give much of it away. All good ideas I'm sure, but not what the three foolish youths planned to spend all their coin on, for there were of course no tellys and cars long ago. Instead they were going to spend their gold on three things and three things only – on drinking and dicing and playing at cards. And they were so happy thinking about how they would spend all their money on drinking and dicing and playing at cards that they forgot their sworn oath to punish Death. But know that Death had not forgotten them. For the three young men had a problem – how could they move the gold without others seeing it and claiming it for their own?

The three foolish youths decided to wait until nightfall when none could see them carrying away their treasure. But waiting all day can be hungry and thirsty work and so all three drew straws to see who among them would go into the city to fetch some bread and wine, while the other two guarded the gold. Well, as it happens it fell to the youngest to leave, for it was he who drew the shortest straw. But no sooner had he gone than the other two fell to talking and the first said to the second, 'What about all that gold, eh? I'm going to spend my share on drinking and dicing and playing at cards.' But then the second said, 'A fine idea to be sure, but what if we could keep all the gold for just us two? We'd have even more money to spend on drinking and dicing and playing at cards.' The first youth thought that this an even better idea. 'But how?' asked he. 'We are two and two are stronger than one,' said the second, 'so how would it be that when our young friend returns and breaks bread, we leap upon him as if playing at rough and tumble? But then we draw our knives and kill him dead!'

The two foolish youths had been taken by greed, but know that greed is a disease just like the plague, for like the plague it spreads very easily. For the youngest of the lame-brained lads, the one walking to town, was thinking, 'What about all that gold, eh? I'm going to spend all my share on drinking and dicing and playing at cards.' But then he had an idea. 'Hold on,' said he, 'for what if I could keep all of that gold for myself? I'd have even more money to spend on drinking and dicing and playing at cards!' And so it was that he went to an apothecary, what you would call a chemist today, and he bought a goodly poison, for as the apothecary told the youth, just one small drop 'would kill anything in less a while than it takes to run a mile'. Happy with the deadly brew, the young man continued on his way, next buying bread and three large bottles of wine. Then, hiding in an alleyway where none could see his shame, he uncorked two

of the bottles of wine and poured the poison into them!

Well, what more can I say? The deal had been done, there was no going back. For no sooner did the young man return to the oak tree, than the other two drew their knives and killed him dead! But killing a friend can be hungry and thirsty work and so they ate the bread and drank the wine – the poisoned bottles of wine – and both suffered slow and miserable deaths. The murderers were murdered by an already murdered man! For you see, my friends, the bent and twisted old man had been right all along; it was Death the three foolish youths had sought and he had indeed been waiting for them at the bent and twisted tree.

For although they found not Death, not he,
Death found them and claimed all three.

Of the Man who Stole Steam

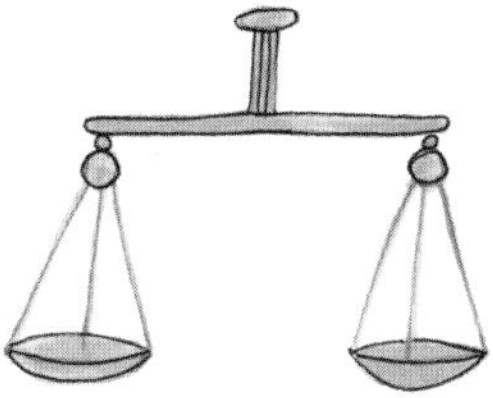

In medieval times the poorest of folk had to rely on the Church for support and also the charity of the rich. But not everyone was willing to share what they had with others… For once long ago there was a cook going about his business, cooking a fine meaty stew to sell to merchants, sailors and pilgrims passing close by. The meaty broth was bubbling and boiling nicely in a great iron pot that stood above a roaring fire, the steam finding the windows and doors of the cook's shop, reaching the noses of all outside. Drawing many of them within, where they would happily pay coin for a bowl of the sweet-smelling stew and also some bread to mop up every last drop.

Well, this day a poor peasant was passing by, a man who laboured hard upon the land, but it was winter; he had no work and so only a few poor pennies to pay for shelter and food. All he had to eat this day was a crust of dry, stale bread, so hard you could use it for hammering iron nails into oak logs. He smelt the beefy broth simmering in the kitchen and so reached in through the window to soften the dry crust in the steam from the stew, making it easier to chew, only wishing he had more money to buy some of the thick meaty soup, but alas this day he did not.

The cook returned to his kitchen and seeing the peasant softening his crust, he roared rude words at the poor man, calling him, 'ROGUE, KNAVE AND VARLET! A GOOD-FOR-NOTHING STEAM-STEALING THIEF!' He grabbed the poor peasant by his ragged gown, demanding he pay for what he'd taken, but of course the poor man could not. 'And anyway,' said the poor peasant, 'why should I, for I have only had the steam and not the stew.'

But the greedy cook would not listen and hauled the poor peasant to prison, there to await judgement in court. The following day the cook and the poor man were brought before the cleverest of court judges, but they could not decide the case. For half of them agreed with the cook, that the sweet-smelling steam was part of the stew, advertising its quality to passers-by, an invitation to all to enjoy its tasty goodness. And so they said that the poor man must pay the cook for what he had taken. But the other learned lords of the law argued that the steam was just waste, saying that the cook had thrown open all his windows and doors to get rid of it. They argued that it was nothing but a nuisance to the cook, that it made him and his servants sweat more than was wanted in a kitchen and that like all steam, it always disappeared into the air. How then could the poor peasant steal that which was no one's to keep?

And so I ask you my friends – how would you bring this squabble to an end? Perhaps you cannot decide, but none could. A final judgement could not be made until a philosopher, a very clever thinker, just happened to be passing by and brought his wit and wisdom to the case. The brainy, brilliant man found favour in both arguments, that it was the cook's steam, but that steam cannot be carried away, and yet still he settled the case. Now I know what you're thinking, my friends: how could he, if both the cook and the poor peasant were right? Well, know this, the poor man was ordered to pay the cook for the steam with his few poor pennies, but the cook could only take the sound of his coins as they fell upon a table. For just as the poor man had only taken the steam and not the stew, so the cook could only take the pennies' pleasing chink and not the coins themselves.

The peasant took steam and the cook spoke a curse,
For all he got in return was the noise from a purse.

Of the Old Woman who Learnt from a Lad

Medieval streets could be muddy mires, especially in winter, when cart wheel and horse hoof churned them all up. But still folk long ago did their best to keep clean… For there was once an old woman who ran a rundown and rickety inn where travellers could pay for a bed, bread and even a hot bath if they were dirty and desired to wash. And all this she did for just two pennies per person, but still her poor inn did little trade.

Well, one day three young merchants stopped at her inn. They were returning from a faraway land where they had made lots of gold and now they wished to rest their saddle-weary bodies, to eat, to drink and to get clean. Each paid two pennies to the old woman and asked her to look after all their gold for safekeeping. And since the gold belonged to all three men, they told the old woman that only all three might ask for it back, saying, 'Do not give it to any one or two of us alone, but only all three of us together.'

The old widow woman agreed and the young men stripped off their grime-stained gowns and climbed into a huge wooden tub full of warm water, large enough to take all three. Each went about the business of bathing, scrubbing his body and washing his hair. And know, my friends, that wealthy men in medieval times often wore their hair long, so two of the three asked the third to go fetch a comb from the old woman, so that they could tease out the tangles from their lustrous long locks.

Now you may be wondering why the third young merchant was so willing to leave his hot bath to fetch the others a comb, but know he was a greedy, grasping man who wanted

all their gold for his own! He asked the old woman for their money, but she remembered the agreement, that she should not give it to any one of them alone and so the old woman said no. And so it was that the false fellow took her to the door of the chamber where his friends were still bathing and called out to them, 'Tell the old woman that she must give me what I wanted.' Well, the two men thought their friend meant the comb and so they replied, 'Old woman, give him what he wants.' And so it was that the old woman was tricked and gave the mean-hearted man all the gold, which quickly he carried away.

After some time the other two grew tired of waiting for the comb and called to the old woman, asking her what had become of their friend? 'He's gone,' said she, 'and he's taken all the coin with him.' Both bathers leapt from the tub, both roaring rude words at the old woman. Quickly they pulled on their gowns over their still damp bodies and dragged the old woman to the court, where a judge found her guilty of giving the gold away and ordered her to pay back their missing coins – if not, the two merchants could take everything else that she owned. The old widow was heartbroken, for all she had left was the six pennies the three men had paid her and so she sat outside the court, weeping and wailing woefully, not knowing what to do.

Then out from the shadows came a small ragged boy who was also alone in the world, a beggar who had nothing to eat. His was a hard life, yet still he smiled upon the world which wished him ill. He put his arm round the old woman's shoulder, asking her what ailed her, what could it be that made her so sad. Having no one else to turn to, she told the small child of the lying merchant and of how she would lose her inn, a rundown, rickety place, but all that she owned in this world. To her surprise the boy laughed loudly, saying, 'Fear not, grandmother. I can help you keep your house and all I want in return is six pence so that I might eat this day and the next.'

Well I ask you, my friends: what would you do in the old woman's place, for she only had six pennies to her name? Would you give them to the beggarly boy, in the hope one so young could help, or would you keep them to buy food for yourself? It's a difficult choice for most, but not for the old woman, for she was as generous as the three wealthy young men were greedy. Willingly she handed the six pennies over to the boy, who in return told her what she must do. 'Go back to the judge,' said the lad, 'and tell him you have brought the two merchants their gold. But,' said he, 'you must tell the judge that if they want payment, they must bring their thieving friend with them, for that was the agreement: that you should not give the gold to any one or two of them alone, but only to all three!'

The old woman had spent her six pennies wisely, for the judge could not argue with the lad's wise words and so decided that she did not have to pay. The poor boy went to live with the old woman and he grew up to become a philosopher, a very clever thinker who you may have already met in the story before this one.

Sixpence bought three men a bath, bread and bed,
While it bought the old woman a poor lad's wise head.

7

In 1381, many an English peasant rebelled against King Richard II, angry at the high taxes they were forced to pay to help fund his wars. The poor people of England had also won many freedoms after the Black Death, because the peasants who survived could now move from one manor to another and charge more money for their work. But the king was trying to stop all that by setting lower wages and making sure the peasants remained as 'serfs', who were forced to live and work for one lord. Led by Wat Tyler and a priest called John Ball, the angry peasants marched on big cities like London. But such was their wrath that violence broke out wherever they went; houses were burned and many people were killed. Even Wat Tyler was cut down by the Lord Mayor of London when he went to meet with the king.

***Wrath**, meaning a rage that cannot be controlled, was thought to be a sin because it often led to feuds, bitter battles that went on for many years. It was also said that wrathful people acted without thinking – saying and doing harm to themselves and others.*

Of the Man who Dealt with the Devil

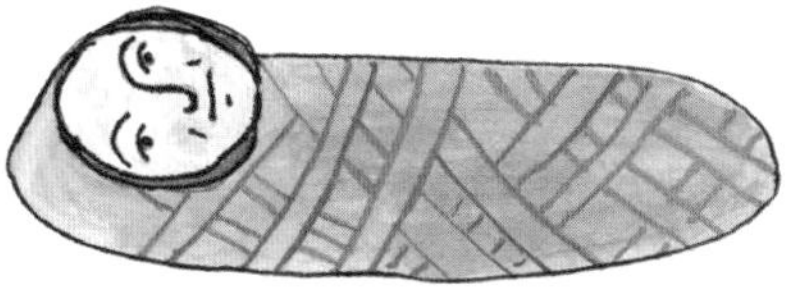

In medieval times there were men called summoners, who summoned wrongdoers to the church courts. But summoners were not well liked, for they could take money from people accused of doing wrong, while some even made up false charges against honest people in order to steal their coin…

For once long ago there was a summoner who rode out early to catch his prey. And as he rode out early that day, happy at all the false charges he would make and the coin he would take, he met a well-dressed man riding upon a horse of huge size: a man wearing a fine gown and a broad-brimmed black hat.

The summoner greeted the stranger kindly, 'Good day,' said he. 'Well met,' replied the stranger in the broad-brimmed black hat, and now the two rode together, talking pleasantly of many things. Soon the summoner thought the stranger was the finest friend he had ever had, for being a summoner and hated by most, he had few friends by which to judge.

After a while the summoner wished to know his new friend's name, where he came from, and how exactly he earned his coin, for by the look of his fair gown and fine horse he was a very wealthy man. The stranger in the broad-brimmed black hat smiled, but not with his eyes. 'I am the Devil!' said he, 'and I live down in Hell, taking the souls of sinners who have done much wrong in this world. And it seems to me,' continued the Devil, 'that we are in the same trade, for we both line our pockets with the misery of others.' The summoner pondered upon the Devil's wise words, for it was true, both took from people all that they did not want to give, which gave him a good idea. 'Why should we not work as one this day?' said the summoner to the Devil, 'and if one of us should get more than the other how about he share it with his new-found friend?' The Devil smiled, but not with his eyes. 'Agreed,' replied he, and they shook hands to seal the deal.

And so it was that the two continued on their journey, going about their bad business, the summoner taking oh-so-much coin from those who had oh-so-little to give. But the Devil he took nothing, he took nowt, and the summoner grew weary, for it was he who would have to share all his earnings with the Devil.

But then he heard the screams and shouts of an old woman who was being pulled by a pig that she held upon a rope. The pig dragged the old woman this way, it dragged the old woman that way, and the only way the pig would not drag the old woman was the way she wished to go! Finally she could bear it no longer. 'The Devil take you, pig,' cried the angry old woman, 'chitterlings, trotters and all!' Well, hearing these words, the summoner called to the Devil, 'Quick, my friend, take the pig, for the old woman says that it's yours. Take it now!' The Devil smiled, but not with his eyes. 'Alas I cannot,' replied he, 'for the old woman spoke in anger and did not mean it with her heart. For the pig provides piglets and without

it she would starve.' And the Devil spoke truthfully, for when the summoner looked again the old woman was playfully tickling the wayward beast behind its ears.

And so it was that the two continued on their journey, going about their bad business, the summoner taking oh-so-much coin from those who had oh-so-little to give. But the Devil he took nothing, he took nowt, and the summoner grew irked, for it was he who would have to share all his earnings with the Devil.

But then he heard a small child crying and saw that the young woman holding it also had tears in her eyes. Both mother and baby were bawling for all to hear, the louder the cries of the one, the louder the replies of the other. Until finally the mother could bear it no longer. 'The Devil take you, child,' yelled the angry young woman, 'sobs, wails, screams and all!' Again the summoner called to the Devil, 'Quickly, my friend, take the baby, for its mother has offered it to you. Take it now!' The Devil smiled, but not with his eyes. 'Alas I cannot,' replies he, 'for the baby's mother spoke in anger and did not mean it with her heart. She would rather give her own life than that of her beloved child.' And the Devil spoke truthfully, for when the summoner looked again the baby had quietened in its mother's arms as she gently rocked it to sleep.

And so it was that the two continued on their journey, going about their bad business, the summoner taking oh-so-much coin from those who had oh-so-little to give. But the Devil he took nothing, he took nowt, and the summoner grew vexed, for it was he who would have to share all his earnings with the Devil.

But then he heard the whinnying of many a horse and saw a cart loaded high with hay, stuck fast in the mud where the track crossed a stream. The carter atop the cart was laying about his horses with a whip that cracked loudly, while he shouted louder still, until finally he could bear it no longer. 'The Devil take you,' cried the angry carter, 'horses, cart and hay, take it all!' Well, the summoner near fell from his horse for he knew a bargain when he heard it. 'Quickly, my friend,' says he, 'the carter has given you everything. Take it now!' Yet again the Devil smiled, but not with his eyes. 'Alas I cannot,' replies he, 'for the carter spoke in anger and did not mean it with his heart. Carting hay is his business and without it his family would suffer.' And the Devil spoke truthfully, for when the summoner looked again the horses had pulled the cart free and all continued merrily on their way.

And so it was that the two continued on their journey, although not merrily like the carter, for although the summoner took oh-so-much coin from those who had oh-so-little to give, still the Devil took nothing, he took nowt, and now the summoner was angry that he would have to share all his earnings that day. 'It seems to me,' says he, 'that you need some lessons in the way of our business, so I will show you how it's done.' He took the Devil to the house of a poor woman who had done nothing wrong, yet still the summoner beat hard upon her door, threatening her with court if she did not pay him silver coin. But the old woman had seen too many hard winters to be worried by a cruel man such as he. She could bear it no longer and threw open her door. 'Enough,' cried the angry old woman. 'The Devil take you, summoner, body and soul!'

Well, my friends, what more can I say? For upon hearing her words, the Devil smiled

broadly, this time with his eyes! 'Now there was someone who meant it with all her heart!' said he, and with that the Devil grabbed the summoner by his hair, stuffed him into one of his saddlebags, and rode quickly back to Hell.

The Devil galloped high into the air,
Then down to his home, a pit of despair.

Of the Wolf in the Well

Some medieval people called out to the Devil when they were angry, while others cried out to wild creatures to help rid them of their wrath… For once there was a farmer who was early about his business, turning the hard, heavy earth over with a wooden plough, pulled by two young oxen. The two animals were new to the work and so pulled the plough this way and pulled it that, but never once did they pull it straight as the poor farmer wished they would.

Eventually the farmer grew angry and could bear it no longer. 'The wolves take you, oxen,' cried he, 'horns, hides and hoofs!' But he had been heard by a wild and wicked wolf who waited and watched all day until the farmer unhitched the oxen from his plough and began to lead them home. And now the baying beast howled loudly, leaping onto the path so that the poor farmer could not pass, saying, 'Where are you going with my oxen?' The farmer was frightened, but still disagreed, although he was respectful as anyone dealing with a wolf should always be. 'Sir,' said he, 'you are mistaken, for these are my oxen and not yours, so I humbly ask that you move aside and let me continue on my way.' But the wild wolf grew angry. 'Have you already forgotten,' roared he, 'what you said while ploughing yon field? I'll remind you, "The wolves take you, oxen, horns, hides and hoofs," and now I've come to claim my prize.'

Yet still the petrified poor farmer would not give in to the wolf's demands, and such was the quarrel between them that it reached the ears of a fox called Reynard, who some of you may have already met in this book. A cunning creature who had eaten very little the past few days, save only for a small piece of cheese and a mouthful of cockerel feathers, Reynard crept out from beneath a nearby bush and spoke clear for both to hear. 'Stop all your fighting on this fair and fine evening,' said he, 'for I am wise and I will judge your case.' And now Reynard listened in a learned fashion to both farmer and wolf, nodding his head knowingly as both did speak. And then he took the farmer to one side, telling the poor man that he would help him if he was willing to pay Reynard two hens, one for him and one for his wife. 'I will pay you two hens *each*,' says the desperate farmer, 'and four more to feed your young pups if you will help me keep my oxen this day.' Having got the farmer to pay him eight hens, the fox told the wolf a very different tale. 'Know,' says Reynard, 'that the farmer has agreed to give you a huge cheese the size of a cartwheel and as heavy as a horse, if you let him keep his oxen.'

Well, foxes like cheese, but wolves love it even more and so he agreed to let the farmer and his oxen depart in peace. Then the fox and the wolf went to fetch the cheese.

'Follow me,' says Reynard, 'for the farmer has told me where it's hidden.' As the sun went down and the moon took over, he led the wolf through a thick forest, where the gnarled and knotted trees loomed large in the darkness. On and on they walked until at last the fox brought the wolf to a deep dark well and told him to look inside. Peering into the damp darkness, the wolf howled with delight, for there at the bottom was a great cheese as big as a cartwheel and as heavy as a horse, or so the wolf thought, for he was only half as clever as the fox and far less quick-witted than all of you.

For if you haven't guessed already, it was the reflection of the moon that the wolf saw down below, but thinking it cheese he wanted it all to himself. But wolves fear water and so he ordered Reynard to fetch the cheese for him, which he willingly did. The cunning creature climbed into one of the two buckets in the well, one tied to each end of a rope. 'Lower me down, friend wolf,' says Reynard as slowly he sank to the bottom. The wolf licked

his lips, drooling at the thought of the tasty treat to come and soon he grew impatient, angry even, for the fox was taking his time. 'Tarry no longer,' howled the wolf, which in medieval times, meant 'Hurry up!' But Reynard called back, 'The cheese is the size of a cartwheel and as heavy as a horse. It's too big for me to lift all alone. And so come down, friend wolf,' says he, 'for together we will soon heave it out!'

Well know, my friends, that anger can blind both man and beast as much as if they had lost both their eyes, and the wrathful wolf did not see the danger as he leapt into the other bucket tied to the rope. For as he went down, the fox flew up, leaping out and leaving his enemy trapped in the well. And I would like to have seen the face of the next person who went to fetch water, but brought up a bucket of wet and wild wolf instead.

The farmer lost hens for words spoken in haste,
But the wolf also suffered, soaked up to his waist.

Of the Knight who Grieved for his Greyhound

Medieval noblemen loved to go hunting with expensive falcons upon their arm and costly dogs by their side… For once there lived a knight who was a spendthrift, a man who loved to spend coin. He bought only the best of food for his table and many fine gifts for his wife. He spent gold on richly embroidered gowns and engraved armour, and a fortune on hunting hawks and hounds.

The knight was warned by his family to stop wasting money, but he would not listen. Eventually he was made poor by his lavish spending and he and his wife had to leave the great city and their comfortable way of life. They moved to a poor country cottage of wood and wattle, earth and clay. So small was their new house that they were forced to leave most of their belongings behind, all those fine things that had not already been sold to pay back all the money they owed.

The knight sold his wife's jewels, his armour and all of his animals, except for one fair falcon and a fine young greyhound, for where once he had hunted for the pleasure, now he must hunt to eat, riding out with his falcon which he used to kill pigeon, crane and goose, and also his young greyhound which he used to run down hare, deer and boar. Both were the knight's most prized possessions, for both caught him lots of game. But the greyhound soon became more than a belonging to be bought and sold, for soon the dog became his loyal companion and faithful friend. You see, the knight was lonely while on the hunt, but the dog kept him company and was well trained, clever and quick. He always came to his master's call and brought down every hare, deer and

boar that he chased. Each night, he would lie by his master's feet dozing by the fire, but always with an eye and ear open to danger, growling low if strangers passed close by. And when his master grew tired, the greyhound would sleep at the end of his bed, keeping both the knight and his wife safe 'til dawn.

Know, my friends, that the knight loved that devoted dog, trusting it with the life of his family, for eventually his wife had a baby boy who was more precious to them than any rich jewel they had left behind in the great city. Things had never been better for the family; the boy was healthy and strong and the knight loved him dearly, so too his simple way of life. There was nothing he enjoyed more than sitting with his son upon his knee, with his wife by his side and his faithful greyhound by his feet, while all of them watched the sun set over forest, field and gently flowing stream. In winter, he would play with both his son and greyhound by the fire, as his wife blew a simple melody upon a bone pipe, the baby laughing loudly as his faithful greyhound rolled over on his back and howled in time with the tune!

But then one day bad news reached the knight's wife, that her sister in the city was ill. She would have to leave early the next morning to visit her sister, leaving her husband and son at home. But there was little food in the house so the knight would have to go hunting and yet he could not leave his baby boy all alone. And so he decided to leave his greyhound at home, taking only his falcon to hunt. For such was his trust in the dog, he knew it would protect the child until his return.

But know, my friends, that in a dark crevice set within an old stone tower, a large snake stirred, roused from its sleep by the creaking cart that carried the knight's wife to town. The wicked wyrm slithered from its dark, dank lair and, attracted by the cries of the baby, it glided into the knight's poor cottage. It drew closer and closer to the baby's low cradle, opening its mouth wide, making ready to strike. But the greyhound, who had been sleeping in the kitchen, suddenly awoke, the hairs on his back bristling as he sensed that all was not well. He sprang from his place by the fire and ran quickly into his master's bedchamber, leaping upon the cruel creature, shaking it this way and that, while the snake fought back, wrapping itself around the dog, sinking its fearsome fangs deep into his back. The fight between dog and snake was long and wild and during the battle the cradle was knocked over so that the baby fell and was trapped underneath. But eventually the brave greyhound got the better of his enemy, tearing the snake to pieces, casting what little was left into the far corner of the bedchamber, where it lay in the dark out of sight.

It was not long after that the knight returned from the hunt and found his faithful hound still wild-eyed and weary from the battle, his muzzle and fur covered in blood. Running into the bedchamber, the knight saw the upturned cradle, but no sign of his son and so he thought that the greyhound had killed his beloved boy. The devoted dog wagged his tail, standing on his hind legs, placing his front paws upon his master's chest, hoping for praise for saving the baby's life. But the knight pushed him away, for such was his anger at the loss of his child, such was his wrath, that he drew his sword and killed his hound with one blow!

Well, it was then that the baby, still hidden beneath the cradle, began to cry and his father found him lying there. Picking up the child and holding him close, the knight followed the trail of blood and found also the dead snake. Realising what he had done, that he had slain the heroic hound that had saved his son, that he had killed his faithful friend, the knight fell to his knees and wept bitter tears and he did not stop crying until darkness fell and his wife returned home. He buried his devoted dog in a pretty place, near meadow and stream, and visited his grave every day. And know, my friends, that the knight never smiled again.

The greyhound was faithful, fearless and brave,
Yet still he was slain and sent to the grave.

8

The End

In the year 1485 Henry Tudor won the Battle of Bosworth, taking the crown of England from King Richard III, who was killed during the fighting that day. Henry's victory marked the end of the Wars of the Roses, fought between two rival branches of the royal House of Plantagenet: the House of Lancaster and the House of York. He became Henry VII, the first Tudor king of England, and his reign marks the end of medieval times and also the end of this book.

And so, my friends, let us finish with a tale about a woman who committed all seven deadly sins…

Of the Rich Woman Buried in Boots

Medieval people really enjoyed a good ghost story, although they called them phantoms, wraiths and spectral visions, messengers who came back from the grave to teach others to be good, God-fearing folk… For once long ago there was a wicked woman who was full of anger, jealousy and desire. A lazy, vain woman who was as mean as she was rich, such was her greed that she kept all of her coin and her food for herself, sharing it with no one save only her closest family and even they did not get as much as they hoped.

But one day the rich woman fell sick and soon she would die. She lay upon her deathbed tossing and turning, whispering and whimpering, and, calling her family to her, made them promise, made them swear upon their lives, that she would be buried in a brand new pair of stout, sturdy shoes, more suited to the feet of a hard-working farmer than a rich noblewoman like her. It was as if she knew something that her family did not, yet it was a story she would never tell. For the wicked woman died and although her family thought it a strange request, she was buried with her feet wrapped in shiny new leather.

But the following evening a knight was riding out late when he heard screams upon the road and saw the mean-hearted woman being chased by a hellish huntsman and his hounds who howled horribly, barking and baying as they came. It was the Devil himself upon a fiery steed, a heinous and horrifying horse. The knight drew his sword and took hold of the wild woman, trying to protect her, wrapping her long blonde hair about his left arm, while he fought off the Devil with his right. But such was the greedy woman's fear, that if all the leaves on all the trees in all the world were to become as tongues, still there would not be enough to speak of her terror. She broke free from the knight, tearing the hair from her head, leaving it wrapped about his arm, her new boots sinking deep into the earth and kicking up stones as she ran from the muddy track into the trees. But the Devil galloped past the knight and grabbed hold of the wailing woman, casting her across his horse, taking her from that dark place, to somewhere much darker still.

The knight told all who would listen of all that he had seen upon the road, but everyone laughed at him, thinking him nowt but a fool. And so it was that he went with spade and lantern to the churchyard and set to digging at the dead woman's grave. The knight dug deep into the dark, dank earth until at last his spade struck the wooden lid of her coffin. And when at last he opened it up, can you guess what he found?

Well know, my friends, that there lay the dead woman, looking as if she were sleeping, but much of her hair was missing and her new leather boots were covered in mud.

The rich woman was greedy, wanting all of
the wealth,
But all she got was a coffin to keep to
herself.

Glossary

ailment – sickness
alas – unfortunately
alchemy – chemistry
ale – type of beer
astrology – study of how the movement of the stars affects people
bade – ordered
bartering – swapping one thing for another
base-born – born into a poor or bad family
base wrought – cheaply made
beguiling – cheating
boils – swellings filled with pus
brag – boast
broth – thick meat, or vegetable soup
bulbous – fat
callous – cruel
cankers – ulcers

caresses – cuddles
chided – told off
chitterlings – cooked pig's intestines
chivalrous – well-mannered and kind
conceited – very proud
coney – a rabbit, but also a nickname for a silly person
conman – trickster
contagions – diseases
covetous – a jealous and greedy person
coxcomb – the fleshy growth on a chicken's head
crackbrained – foolish
crone – an old woman
crusades – religious wars
dearth – lack of something
deluge – huge flood
devour – eat quickly
dwell – to live somewhere
feats – things done with strength and courage
fleecing – cheating
forged – metal that has been heated, hammered and shaped
harken – listen
heed – take notice

heinous – evil
idle – lazy
irked – annoyed
keep – large and usually square tower set within castle walls
knave – a dishonest person
lame-brained – foolish
largesse – generosity
learned – well educated
manor – land owned by a lord
maul – a hammer
meagre – small
mean – poor and also small
mellow – soft and gentle
merchants – people who buy and sell things
mire – boggy ground
mock – to laugh at, or something that is fake
monarch – a king or queen
moonstruck – unable to act normally
munificence – generosity
nobles/noblemen – members of powerful families who helped rule the land
oaths – promises
paled – went white with fear

peasant – a poor person who worked on the land
pilgrim – a person who visits religious sites
purge – to make someone vomit or poo!
putrid – rotten
ramshackle – falling down
rapscallion – a naughty person or joker
rascal – a naughty or dishonest person
realm – a kingdom ruled over by a monarch
rogue – a dishonest person
sage – a wise person
scoundrel – a dishonest person
slew – killed
smite – to hit hard
sovereign – a king or queen
thither and yon – here and there
tithe – one tenth of all produced by farmers that had to be paid to the Church
tyrant – a cruel ruler
varlet – a dishonest person
vexed – annoyed
withered – shrivelled with age
woe – sadness
wooing – trying to win the love of another

wyrm – a dragon or snake
yokel – a foolish country person

Bibliography

Aldington, R., *Boccaccio: The Decameron*, 2 vols (Folio Society, 1955)

Appelbaum, S., *Medieval Tales and Stories* (Dover Publications Inc., 2000)

Bett, H., *English Legends* (B.T. Batsford Ltd, 1950)

Brewer, D., *Medieval Comic Tales* (Cambridge, 1972)

Chilton, P.A., *The Heptameron* (Penguin Classics, 1984)

Crowlesmith, Revd J., *Wonder Tales of the Middle Ages* (London, 1932)

DuVal, J. & Eichmann, R., *Fabliaux Fair and Foul* (Medieval Texts & Studies, 1992)

Edmonds, I.G., *Trickster Tales* (J.B. Lippincott and Co., 1966)

Hartland, E.S., *English Fairy and Other Folk Tales* (London, 1890)

Harvey, F.J., *A Wonder Book of Old Romance* (Darton and Co., *c.*1907)

Joynes, A., *Medieval Ghost Stories* (Boydell Press, 2001)

Klaf, F.S. & Hurwood, B.J., *A Hundred Merry Tales* (The Citadel Press, 1964)

Komroff, M., *Tales of the Monks from the Gesta Romanorum* (New York, 1936)

Matthews, J. & Stewart, B., *Tales of Arthur: Adventure Stories from Arthurian Legend* (Javelin Books, 1988)

Mayne, W., *The Hamish Hamilton Book of Heroes* (Hamish Hamilton Ltd, 1967)

Millar, M.J., *Knights, Beasts and Wonders* (New York, 1969)

Ohlgren, T.H., *A Book of Medieval Outlaws: Ten Tales in Modern English* (Sutton Publishing, 2000)

Osborne, M. & Howell, T., *Favourite Medieval Tales* (Scholastic Inc., 1999)

Picard, L., *Hero Tales from the British Isles* (Penguin Books, 1963)

Robbins, R.H., *The Hundred Tales: Les Cent Nouvelles Nouvelles* (Crown Publishers Inc., 1960)
Speed, P., *Medieval Cautionary Tales* (Italica Press, 2003)
Storer, E., *Il Novellino: The Hundred Old Tales* (G. Routledge & Sons Ltd, *c.*1925)
Westwood, J., *Medieval Tales* (Rupert Hart-Davis Ltd, 1967)
Wright, D., *Geoffrey Chaucer, The Canterbury Tales* (Oxford University Press, 1985)

Society *for* Storytelling

Since 1993, The Society for Storytelling has championed the ancient art of oral storytelling and its long and honourable history – not just as entertainment, but also in education, health, and inspiring and changing lives. Storytellers, enthusiasts and academics support and are supported by this registered charity to ensure the art is nurtured and developed throughout the UK.

Many activities of the Society are available to all, such as locating storytellers on the Society website, taking part in our annual National Storytelling Week at the start of every February, purchasing our quarterly magazine Storylines, or attending our Annual Gathering – a chance to revel in engaging performances, inspiring workshops, and the company of like-minded people.

You can also become a member of the Society to support the work we do. In return, you receive free access to Storylines, discounted tickets to the Annual Gathering and other storytelling events, the opportunity to join our mentorship scheme for new storytellers, and more. Among our great deals for members is a 30% discount off titles from The History Press.

For more information, including how to join, please visit

www.sfs.org.uk